MIRACULOUS WAYS *to* CONQUER CANCER

AWAKEN TO THE POWER OF HEALING WITHIN YOU

RYUHO OKAWA

IRH Press

Contents

⌒CHAPTER TWO⌒

Miraculous Healing Power

ᏟᎪ CHAPTER THREE ᏬᎧ

Ways to Make Cancer Vanish

1. Curing Illnesses is the Royal Road of Religion

2. Why are there People who Get Cancer?

3. A Mental Attitude to Fight Illnesses

4. How to Make Cancer Vanish

᥎ CHAPTER FOUR ᥏

Spiritual Readings of Diseases – Q&A Sessions

Preface

Many modern people are distressed and suffer from illnesses. Also, the more medical science progresses, the more types of illnesses emerge. In addition, as the average life-span increases, the number of intractable and rare diseases increases. Among them, there are even people who have become a "department store of diseases."

However, there is only one truth. Although at a slow pace, human bodies are continuously changing, just like the flow of a river; human bodies cannot remain in the same form. The power of the mind can rebuild your body. Moreover, as that happens, faith begins to work as an immense power. In the name of faith, you should envision an ideal image of yourself. Including cancer, there are countless amounts of cases in which "fatal diseases," as told by medical science, were cured.

Believe, and you shall be saved. Ask, and it shall be given you.

Ryuho Okawa
Founder and CEO of the Happy Science Group
December 28, 2010

Chapter One

The Secret Key
To Recovering Your Health

Lecture given on March 1, 2009
at Tokyo Shoshinkan
Tokyo, Japan

1
Underlying Causes of Illness

Illness is a manifestation of excuses or discontents
Of the current situation

In this chapter entitled, "The Secret Key to Recovering Your Health," I would like to talk about health issues, mainly from religious perspectives while referring to my book, *Cho Zettai Kenkoho* [The Way to Definite Health] (Tokyo: IRH Press, 2009).

In modern day Japan, with progression in medical science, vast amount of sick people are being treated in hospitals. However, the number of sick people is also increasing at the same time. This indicates how various illnesses will keep emerging as the field of medicine continues to progress. In short, as research progresses further, categories of illnesses will further increase and when the name of the disease is announced, it will start to seem as though the illness really exists.

As for people who are receiving treatment at hospitals, they seem to feel relieved and be at ease when they receive diagnoses and are given names for their conditions. When people are approved of being sick, they no longer need to feel as though they have to be "who they think they are supposed to be." In this sense, it can be said that it is as though they have received a certificate from the doctor.

Put simply, when people have some kind of illness, it offers them an extremely favorable reason to accept that they are not in perfect condition or in their desirable state.

Although it may be common sense to think that nobody will feel pleased to be ill, in real life, this is not always the case. If you go to big hospitals and listen to the conversations elderly people have when they walk past each other at the corridors, the reality is that you will hear them bragging to each other about the kind of illness they have rather than words of greeting. You often hear them boast about which among them has the most serious sickness, which of them has been hospitalized for longer and which of them have heavier symptoms with a higher risk of dying.

In addition, heavier symptoms act as warning signs for the patient's family, the ones who should be worried and concerned, alerting them for the lack of love that they are receiving. It appears as if they are saying, "I am suffering from this illness right now because all of you have neglected your duties toward me as my children [or grandchildren]."

Hence, following is the point I would like to make. Essentially, no one would be pleased at becoming ill, but in reality there are people who are trying to make a plea through their illnesses. What is this plea? Their illness is a form of excuse or discontent directed toward their family, society or colleagues for not being engaged in work of social recognition or for not being placed in an admirable position.

There are number of cases in which the severity of their illness is often used as an expression to say, "I am actually in this state because of all of you." This is something we need to be careful of.

Of course, there are also many people who are in hospitals for the time being because they have grown old and have nowhere else to go. Just as though little children go to kindergarten or nursery school, when people reach a certain age it is often the case that hospitals become a safer place to be in; they can be taken care of if they should happen to fall ill or pass away. For this reason, in many cases elderly people enter hospitals before it is really necessary. In a way, hospitals are becoming like kindergartens for the elderly.

However, what I want to say is this; it would be better to reflect and rethink upon this way of thinking for once.

Humans are beings with the car And the driver in a single entity

It is fine for medical science to develop, but the fundamental philosophy of Western medicine is completely based on materialism; it considers this world to be exclusively material-based.

In Western medicine, they research on the relationships between material substance; in other words, on the relationship between "medicine as a material substance" and the "human body as a material substance." They are observing from the perspective of whether medicine as a material substance has an effect on the human body as a material substance.

The human body in such situation tends to be treated more like "a type of machine." Their main focus is the idea that "illness is like mechanical failure, so unless we replace the broken part or do some kind of repairs, the machine will not get better." This situation is similar to a garage where cars are repaired. Hospitals carry out all kinds of checks from the perspective to see if any "parts" have worn out or whether the "power line" and the "frame of the car" are damaged. Then they will repair or replace any of the damaged parts. Instead of putting gasoline, they use intravenous drips. This is the way things have become. People are being treated as if they are cars.

Certainly, we cannot disagree to this aspect completely. However, as I have stated time and time again, the body in which human beings think of as "themselves" is nothing more than a vehicle. There is nothing wrong with people regarding their own body as a car, but your body is merely a vehicle and your true nature is the driver himself. I want you all to remember this.

The quality of the car itself is not necessarily the only thing that is associated with whether or not you are a good driver. You are not driving your car solely for the purpose to enter and win prizes in a car race. In most cases, the cars that you are driving are ordinary vehicles that are common everywhere in the world. It is good enough if it does what it needs to do, like taking you to the next town. Whether you are a good driver or not determines whether you get into an accident or not.

You are not driving an ultra-high performance car that can avoid every accident. Your car does not have the luxury of automatically detecting danger and avoiding it; if you fall asleep at the wheel you are bound to bump into other cars or houses. Also, if the driver is drunk, without a doubt, the person will not be able to drive according to traffic regulations. This is an obvious fact.

Thus, although it is fine to have some interest in the car itself, the perceptiveness of the person, such as his attentiveness, judgment, soundness and wisdom, is of vital importance to live a healthy life. Even if you were not given a physical body of high-caliber from your parents, it is still possible to get through a lifetime without any accidents if you drive carefully. I would like you to be aware of this as a prerequisite. Especially in cases of hereditary illnesses where the body was born with some unhealthy condition, it definitely suggests that there was some defect on the car, or the body.

However, even if there are no congenital disorders, the body becomes more vulnerable to damage after middle age. Although it is a little hard to define when middle age begins since some would be pleased while others would feel angry, generally speaking, the body becomes more vulnerable to damage after the age of 35. From then on, we need to receive periodical checks and maintenance in order to ensure that the body is functioning properly and that nothing is faulty. This can be said as a matter of common sense.

All of this is the general way of thinking as an introductory portion of this chapter. First, I would like for you to be aware that "a human is not merely a car but a being living its life with both the driver and the car together as one."

2
The Mind Creates Illness

The energy to live is the true identity of the mind

I previously stated that humans are beings with the car and the driver in a single entity. It may sound old-fashioned or dignified to say that this driver is actually the soul or the spirit part of us, so to put it more simply, we could call it the "mind." Many people would understand if I were to say that "human beings consist of a mind and a body." If I call it the "mind," more than 90% of people would understand.

However, as soon as they hear that humans "consist of a spirit and a body," about half the people will start feeling uneasy and start to question if such a thing is acceptable. But this is solely to do with the choice of words. In fact, the true identity of the soul or the spirit, in a worldly sense, is what we usually call the "mind."

The mind remains invisible so long as we live in this world, but we are all aware that it exists. We must have all sensed that something like the mind is there. I don't think there is anyone who feels as though his own body functions by clockwork or feel as if our hands extend like a magic robot hand when we reach out to grab something.

You may have toys at home, but I'm sure you don't feel like a toy when you move yourself. Something should feel different. Robot dogs have come onto the market, but I'm sure you can tell the difference between a robot dog and the pet dog that you own at home. The fact that they both move, have similar habits and the fact that they bark and respond to words may be what they have in common, but a robot dog and a real dog is different. The difference is whether there is life dwelling inside or not. In the same way, the difference between a robot, or a simple machine, and a living human being, is whether they can feel the existence of the mind or not.

Expressed in a different word, this "mind" is in fact "life." The true essence of life is the mind. It is living energy. To further express it in a different way, it is the energy to live. This is the true identity of the mind. It is the energy that keeps trying to pour life into the physical body. It is the leading character and the ruler of the body. It is the strong will or the strong intent that thinks and constructs plans of the kind of life that it will lead using the body. This is, in fact, the true identity of the "mind."

The mind has the ability to create new things

Medical scientists and biologists often consider the "mind" as the "workings of the brain." However, in actual fact, the mind is different from brain functions. The brain is considered to be playing a role of a computer. Although computers are becoming closer to human beings in their abilities, there is a certain limit as to how close a computer can become more like us. This is because computers have their own creators. Human beings created computers. There is always someone who programs the computer in the way that he wants it to function. Human beings invented computers. So, this makes human beings God-like existences for computers.

Then, for human beings, what would be the existence equivalent to the one who created computers? From a religious point of view, this would be God, Buddha or the wisdom of the great universe. This is expressed in a number of ways. Human beings were created by a tremendous power from a distant world that transcends far beyond this world. Hence, just as human beings created computers, it is plausible to think that a mighty power is at work with us, aimed at guiding humans to live with a purpose.

Furthermore, what would be the difference between computers and the mind? The human mind owns creativity. This is the ability to create, the ability to create new things, the ability to come up with new ideas. Humans are able to do more than to just simply repeat and reiterate matters that were prepared in advance; we are able to create the future by producing new thoughts for new subjects and problems. We are able to find solutions for things that are yet unknown and produce ideas. This is the kind of creativity that the human mind possesses.

In addition to the power to create, the human mind possesses the ability of imagination. This is the fundamental difference between the human mind and computers. The human mind not only responds to what has been inputted but has the power to go over and above to create new things based on what has been inputted. It is in this sense that human beings are said to be the "children of God" and that they were "made in the image of God." Human beings are mighty beings that have the power to create new things, as well as the power to produce new ideas. It is for this reason that humans are said to be the children of God and a part of God dwells inside each and every one of them.

To elaborate on the mind more precisely, a spirit body that is roughly the same size as the physical body dwells inside each of us and the core part that controls the other parts is what we call the "mind." This part mainly governs our will and our feelings. It is this part, the mind, that actually draws in a type of spiritual energy from God, Buddha, high spirits and so on in the heavenly realm. It is the identity of what is keeping us connected to them.

When humans are deeply moved or go through a spiritual experience, warmth wells up from within their hearts. This does not only happen on an individual level; this can also happen when a group of people in the same place are deeply moved at the same time. This is the spiritual light, the spiritual energy from the heavenly realm. This means that this spiritual energy is flowing from the heavenly realm into various people at various places at the same time. As a matter of fact, human beings are like a group at the downstream of this energy flow that is coming down from the high spirits of the heavenly world. This is the essence of human beings. In this sense, we may say that humans are extremely noble beings. Humans possess a portion of an element similar to Buddha and the God.

The mind creates illness
When creativity functions as destructivity

As the mind has the ability to create, it would of course mean that it has the ability to destroy. What does it mean to destroy? This is the part that corresponds to so-called "illness." Humans can destroy their own bodies by means of their own mind. We can provoke various kinds of malfunctions and create sicknesses.

The body is very much under the sway of the material world but when the mind is inclined in a disharmonious direction, changes will start to occur to the body. If the phenomenon is low-key, it will go no further than the level of "feeling out of shape." But if it intensifies, pathological lesion will occur, followed by an illness. This can be cancer or other serious illnesses. Illness will appear in various ways and it will manifest in the weakest part of the person's body.

In the book, *The Way to Definite Health* [as already cited], I have described it as follows, by using a metaphor of a river. "The physical body is just like a flowing river. Just as it overflows at the parts where there are breaks in its banks, illnesses appear in parts where the body is weak. A certain illness will appear because that part of the body is weak. Even if the illness is cured, another illness will appear elsewhere as long as there is disharmony in the mind. This is the kind of relationship the mind and the body has."

There are many types of illnesses and, medically speaking, there are various medicines and remedies that are said to be effective for each illness. There are a number of treatments available. However, if we trace things back to the roots, the matter is actually very simple. It is the disharmony in the mind that is causing the illness and it appears at the weakest part of the body. In some cases the illness appears at the weakest part of the body at the present moment, after it being used for a long time. There are also cases when a certain part of the body is weak from birth and an illness appears in that part. Either way, disharmony will manifest as a phenomenon in the weakest part of the body, thereby becoming an illness.

In this way, the mind is able to create illnesses; however, this is our creativity functioning in a negative way, different from the original sense of creativity. Hence, this can be seen as the destructivity or the destructive power that the mind has. You all possess this ability. With almost no exception, you all possess the ability to create illnesses. It is as if you all possess half the power of God. However, you must not forget to exert the other half of this power, which would be to "cure illness." If we are able to create illnesses, we must be able to cure illnesses through the same ability.

Generally speaking, in most cases, an illness would mean to develop impairment to one of our internal organs, our brain or our vascular system. However, our internal organs don't stay exactly the same all year round. All cells replace themselves within a year. The same goes for our bones. None of the bones remain the same all year round. Even the skull replaces itself. The blood vessels and the blood, of course, are replaced too. There is nothing in your body that remains the same as the previous year. It probably looks very much the same from the outside, but the body has replaced itself entirely.

Therefore, if we take the stomach as an example, in the case of stomach cancer, the body has to keep on creating a malignant focus around the stomach area. The body has to be in an ongoing state of continual destruction on the stomach. Through the continuation of such cycle, a particular illness takes shape.

In contrary, however, if we are able to create malignant things in our cells through such manner, to think of changing them into good things will enable us to do so as well.

If we take our time,
We can move involuntary muscles with our will

You have probably learned in your science lesson that the human body is made up of muscles that can be moved by surface consciousness [voluntary muscle] and some parts that cannot be moved [involuntary muscle]. For instance, the muscles in your arm are voluntary which means they can be moved by your own will if you want them to do so.

On the other hand, your heart is an involuntary muscle, so it moves with its own accord without your volition. There are some Indian yoga practitioners who are able to make their hearts start and stop with their own will, but these people are exceptional. It is something that cannot be done by general people. The heart beats by its own accord. In this way, there are parts of the human body that can be moved by our will and the parts that cannot be. However, although involuntary muscles appear as though they cannot be moved by our will, that is actually not the case.

The difference is similar to that of between the agile movements of animals and the slow movements of plants. It is generally thought that plants do not move, but if you film a plant for 24 hours and play it at high speed, you will see that plants are also able to move. Plants too, keep moving and changing. It is simply that their movements are very slow. Animals are alert and are able to run anywhere they want, but plants are unable to, since they do not have any legs.

However, if you keep watching them for one, two and three days, it will be clear to you that they are living creatures. If you film them for long hours and play it back at high speed, you will see the changes. Plants do move. Animals and plants are the same in their willingness to live and the willingness to try and change.

The difference between voluntary and involuntary muscles is similar to the difference between animals and plants. You will be able to move any part of the body that can be moved instantly as you wish. But when it comes to the part that cannot be moved so easily, it probably does not work the same. For example, even if you want to try and change the position of your intestines, they will not move easily. However, if you continuously think long enough, "I'd like to change the position of my intestines, like this," they will very gradually move.

The crystalline lens in the eye would be another example. It is usually said that once this is impaired, our eyesight will not recover. This is because the thickness of this crystalline lens cannot be changed freely by will. Indeed, you may not be able to change it in a course of a day, but you can do it slowly over time. In fact, you have the freedom to do so.

If we were primitive people and not modern-day people and we became short-sighted, for instance, our eyesight would gradually recover with time since we would struggle in our daily life without being able to wear any glasses. It would be impossible for us to survive without the ability to clearly spot our prey, so our eyesight will recover to adapt. However, this can hardly be the case for modern people, since it would be quicker to wear glasses. This causes the crystalline lens to not move around so much.

In this way, I would like you to be aware that the human body possesses the creativity to be free to a certain extent. This is the second level of awareness that all of you must have.

3
Miracles Occur
In Proportion to Your Faith

The Spirit World and this world coexist

I will tell you about the next level of awareness. As I mentioned earlier, there are these two things—the "mind" and the "body." This can also be referred to as the "spirit" and the "physical body." There are two different types—the spirit and the physical body, which can also be expressed as the mind and body. So far, I have taught the mutual relationship between these two. This is also preached in Buddhism.

In Buddhism, this is known as "The mind and matter as one," meaning, "the physical body [matter] and the mind are inseparable, they are in unity." From a Buddhist perspective, the mind and the physical body are neither separate nor joined. What this means is that the mind and body mutually affect one another and do not exist separately. However, there is a way of thinking that goes beyond this which is one level higher.

Even those who believe in the Spirit World tend to think that all things including human bodies or things that are present in this world are temporary and that the other world and this world are separate things. But there is a viewpoint one level higher than this which says that in reality, they are not separate things.

Perhaps this could be stated like the following. Imagine a beaker with muddy water inside. If you stir it, the upper part will gradually start to clear as the mud settles at the bottom. This muddy part, I'm sorry to have to put it this way, is equivalent to three dimensional world where you are all living now, that is, this world. Just as the water gets more limpid and transparent as we look higher up at the beaker, the limpid portion represents the fourth, fifth, sixth dimensions and higher. This is one way of looking at it.

Hence, another way of viewing this would be, "In reality, this world and the other world are not two separate worlds. They are, in fact, the same, but this world is the part where the coarse granular has settled as sediment. This is to say that there is a certain extent to what human beings can see and hear. The worlds beyond the fourth dimension exist outside of this boundary, where humans in this world cannot see nor hear. We live in a dimension of coarse vibration, which is why we can clearly see each other."

In this manner of speaking, the Spirit World and this world simultaneously exist within the same time and space; it is just that the wavelengths of the vibration are different. Only, people who live in the third dimension of coarse wavelength are usually unable to sense it. However, the beings in the other world that possess refined wavelength are able to see the things of this world very clearly. This can be of actual reality. For instance, the human eyes cannot see a moving object that is beyond a certain speed.

According to the UFOs sightings, it has been reported that flying objects suddenly disappear out of sight in an instant. It is generally said that when such phenomena occur, that is when they are flying in the Spirit World and other dimensions. In such manner, another way of thinking about it is that this world and the other world are not two separate worlds but that they coexist; the difference only lies in the state of the existence within each world.

Stated differently, everything is made up of the light of Buddha [God] and because this light of Buddha [God] is extremely refined, there are numerous stages in between before it gradually thickens and reaches a stage where it becomes a big clump. This three dimensional world is where the vibration is at its coarsest and has solidified.

Additionally, it is a mistake to think that there is a physical body apart from the spirit body. This physical body is in fact one of the manifestations of the spirit body. The physical body is viewed as an appearance of the spirit body that has manifested itself in an extremely solidified state. This is the third level of thinking.

The laws of the third dimension will no longer apply
When the higher dimensional power comes into play

To tell the truth, just as the title of this chapter says, "The Secret Key to Recovering Your Health," various kinds of phenomena will start to occur once your enlightenment progresses this far. It is at this point when all the rules of this third dimension start to overturn. For people who think that this world is established as an independent world and the laws in this world do not change at all, so will it be. The reality will project their beliefs.

However, this world is in fact connected to the other world and by understanding the laws of the other world, we are able to change the laws of this world, too. If people realize and grasp this concept, they can change this world.

For example, if a car is the only option we have to drive on the expressway and you want to get ahead of the car in front, there is no alternative but to think about how to overtake that car on the road. However, if you can stand one level above and consider using a helicopter to reach your destination faster, the person who got overtaken will be overwhelmed with the situation and may say, "How did you get here before me? I was driving on the expressway and not even one car passed by me on the way." The person will not be able to understand no matter how much he thinks about it.

Life in the third dimensional world is like driving on the expressway; if a helicopter flies through the air and arrives earlier, people will be overwhelmed and think, "I really do not have a clue how this happened." However, using a helicopter, the same thing will happen no matter how many times we try. Even though no one overtakes you on a car on earth, there is nothing strange or magical if people actually arrive before you; they are just using helicopters and planes.

This is what happens when the laws of the higher dimensions are at work. This kind of thing will happen when people in this world become aware that there are approaches from higher dimensions.

Similarly, trying to combat illnesses by only using the laws of this world such as "matter versus matter," "medicine versus pathological lesions" and "operations versus pathological lesions," it would be the same thing as two cars on the expressway competing against each other to see who will arrive first at the destination.

However, these third dimensional laws will no longer apply when powers from the worlds above come into play. Through such phenomena, various miracles have occurred in many different religions throughout history. This is the same reason why illness can be cured by religion.

Miracles happen when you have strong faith
And the mission to provide proof for miracles

The laws of this world are no longer applied when powers from the higher dimensions get involved. As a prerequisite, a person must have faith and the powerful strength to believe. Additionally, the person must be appropriate for miracles and must be chosen as someone to receive such a miracle.

Miracles do not happen to everyone. A person must have deep faith and be worthy to work miracles. A miracle will occur when both these conditions are met. It is hard knowing what your mission is in life, since it is your own "workbook of life" to solve. However, if you have a mission along the lines of demonstrating proofs for miracles, there is a possibility in recovering from an incurable sickness. Even if the doctor tells you that you will die of it for sure, 100%, there is a possibility in recovering. Strong faith is what is required. Its strength will double for sure if you receive assistive powers and powerful prayers from your fellow Dharma friends who practice the Truth together.

If the following conditions are met, there will be countless situations in the future where the doctors will wonder whether they made some kind of mistake in their thinking: strong feelings from those around the person to be cured as well as a strong feeling in the patient himself. In addition, there is a need for this miracle to occur as proof of the Truth.

However, by law, because doctors are the only ones who are allowed to cure illnesses in Japan, it is considered inappropriate for religious groups to use the words "able to cure." If I were to put it in another way, it would be that illnesses naturally heal by themselves.

With pure faith, participate in ritual prayer and if you have a mission, a calling to provide proof for miracles, you will recover without a doubt. Even if you do not completely recover, it is possible for your life to be prolonged to some extent, so that you do not die during an important stage in life.

Everybody will die someday and it is impossible to avoid it or for us to become immortal. However, all that is required is to live the main stages of your life in good health, so that you are able to work and live for your family. It is important to wish for this.

As I previously stated, if the conditions are met, a power different from that of this world will surely come into play. This will occur in proportion to your faith. Miracles will occur if the following conditions are met: If you can truly believe that the real world is not this world but the other world and that you are born into this temporary world for spiritual training. If you can live your life according to these perspectives and devote yourself to spiritual training every day, that's when miracles, such as curing of illnesses or resolving difficulties and hardships in this world, will occur.

Furthermore, those things will be resolved if you can live your life according to such perspective and devote yourself to spiritual training in diligence on a daily basis.

Everything will appear just as it is envisioned in our minds. Humans are spiritual beings and are able to eventually manifest what we think of in our minds. Therefore, it is important that we train ourselves to strongly envision how and what we would like to become in the future and paint pictures of our future in our minds. Through such discipline, these things will become possible in reality.

So please try to train yourself to strongly envision an image in your mind of how you want to be in the future. Adding faith to it will accelerate the approach to make it a reality, without a doubt.

Any kind of illnesses can be cured. You can cure your illness with this book.

Chapter Two

Miraculous Healing Power

Lecture given on August 11, 2010
at Ueda Local Temple
Nagano, Japan

1

As Your Faith Strengthens, Various Miracles will Begin to Occur

In this chapter, I will speak on the theme of "Miraculous Healing Power." I am sure you would realize that I am currently the world's greatest psychic, if you read a great number of books I have published. At this moment, there is no one in this world that has spiritual powers beyond mine. Therefore, all kinds of miracles will begin to occur if only you, the followers of Happy Science, establish your faith.

In order for all of your faith to be established, it is necessary for you, my followers, to overcome many kinds of obstacles. It is not enough to merely understand the teachings of Happy Science in your head. You need to let it settle to the bottom of your soul.

For example, I am sure you can understand my teachings by reading the words in the three fundamental Laws series—*The Laws of the Sun* (New York: IRH Press, 2013), *The Golden Laws* (New York: Lantern Books, 2011) and *The Nine Dimensions* (New York: IRH Press, 2012).

However, if you take a moment and think, "What if the teachings in these books are true?" I'm sure you will realize that the content of these books are actually quite astonishing. The same goes for all my other books.

If you take my teachings of the spiritual world with strong assurance that they are "the Truth itself," then you should realize just how immense the contents are. It is possible to understand the teachings by reading my books on an intellectual level. However, if you remain satisfied and leave it at that, your understanding will remain superficial and, quite often, the teachings are not absorbed into the deeper levels of your soul.

Last year [2010], I published *The Laws of Creation* (Tokyo: Happy Science, 2010). If you are to ask what the essential teachings of the principle of the spiritual world are, it comes down to the principle of creation. I believe there are people who are already satisfied by only using it as a simple way to receive ideas or inspiration. However, this principle itself is also the power that has been creating the spiritual existence in the Real World. In addition, it is the power that has been creating the lives that human beings go through in this world. You must know this truth.

2

The Physical Body and the Spiritual Body Are Closely Connected

Pain felt before death
Sometimes continues in the other world

The physical body, which is visible, is not the only factor that makes up a human being. We actually have a spiritual existence [spiritual body] that dwells in our physical body; this spiritual existence has a multi-layered structure, just like an onion. The very core is the existence very close to God and Buddha and there are many layers surrounding the core. The closer to the outer surface, the more human-like the layers are.

The most outer layer is called the "astral body" and it is shaped very similar to the human body. This astral body carries the consciousness of all the body parts such as eyes, nose, eyebrows, along with the other parts such as the heart, liver, kidneys and all the other organs. A form that is exactly the same shape as the human body is fitted neatly inside. However, if you were to observe this astral body with spiritual eyes, you would notice that it is somewhat bigger than the physical body and that the astral body appears slightly outside the edge of the physical body.

In most cases, when you take a look at yourself after you return to the other world, you wouldn't look different to how you did in this world. Your appearance would remain the same up to the half-moon of your fingernails; because of this, people sometimes wonder whether they are still alive. In addition, because the astral body, or the outer most layer of the spiritual body, carries the consciousness of the internal organs, there are many cases where those who died of internal organ failures continue to be in pain. The consciousness of the particular organ that failed and caused them to die is still suffering from pain.

Those who are not spiritually awakened or not thoroughly aware that they have died are kept in the same condition as to when they died and the pain in which they had in their body moments before their death continues to follow. This is a truly mysterious sensation. Even pain from an intravenous needle follows the astral body after death. If we are given intravenous drips for a long period of time during hospitalization, our arms will start to hold pain; what's more, this pain can also remain even when we go to the other world after death.

The astral body and the physical body are in contact with each other over a very wide area, so the astral body carries similar sensations as the physical body.

The differences are that the astral body can go

through ceilings and fly in the air. For example, although you do not intend to, sometimes your astral body can be found flying above an ambulance or the hearse that is carrying your physical body, as if you were Superman. This is what happens for some reason.

Another difference is, even if a dead person tries to talk to those who are alive at the vigil or the funeral, they will not be able to hear anything. Here, another greatly mysterious sensation will be experienced. Even if your astral body can hear everything that the attendees, the priest and all the other people are saying, only your voice cannot be heard by anybody else. This state of one-way situation continues.

It is difficult to persuade a materialistic person, Even in the other world

Indeed, sometimes the pain from illnesses and diseases are taken back to the other world. I know this cannot be helped if this is experienced right after death. However, there are people who suffer in the same way for years or even decades after their death. A person who died from stomach cancer continues to suffer from stomach pain. Someone who died from a heart disease continues to feel pain in his heart. One who died from a head injury in a car accident will continue to feel pain in his head for decades. Things like this happen. If such state continues for decades after death, without a doubt, there is something wrong.

If this is the case, it shows their unawareness of the "first level of enlightenment." For example, the person has not awakened to the fact that the true nature of a human being is a spiritual existence. He is not aware of how he is meant to live in the world after death. At some point after such person's death, his deceased relatives and friends, or even Angels of Light, will talk to him about these things. Nonetheless, even though the person listens to what these beings are saying, he will not be able to understand what they are talking about; it will not make sense to him.

This is exactly the same situation as when the followers of Happy Science try to convey about the other world and the spirits to the general public—it doesn't make sense to them. They will not lend an ear to followers' persuasions but instead keep saying, "My stomach hurts even if you say that" or "I am suffering from lung cancer, so there is nothing I can do."

This is particularly true when doctors, who think that illnesses can only be cured at hospitals, die of an illness. They will keep on saying, "There is no medicine, nor can we conduct an operation. So my illness cannot be cured." There will be no hope for salvation. Even the monks in the other world are having difficulty trying to save these people. They wonder if the only way they can persuade those doctors are to appear like a doctor when talking to them.

However, even if they do appear like one, the dead doctors will point out that the "doctors" are frauds because the scalpel is held the wrong way. Even when disguised like nurses, the dead doctors point out the lack of basic manners of nurses and all the other wrongs. It is pretty hard to convince doctors who have died.

In this way, materialism has permeated to a considerable degree. Indeed, there is object existence in this world and science today has adopted the thought that the human body is composed of parts like a car. Therefore, the fundamental way of thinking in the field of medical science is basically made up of beliefs such as, "The broken parts only need to be changed" and "Broken parts need to be repaired." For this reason, it is very difficult for such people to switch their mind to acknowledge that they are now a spiritual existence, even after death.

For those who stubbornly believe in materialism, it is not easy to try and have them understand that materialism is considered "wrong view" in Buddhism. The more stubborn the intellectual person becomes, the harder it will be to convince. Even if you show them a spiritual phenomenon to prove the existence of the spiritual world, such people will interpret it as some kind of hallucination.

In modern-day Japan, there are scientists who state, "God does not exist. It is a figment created by the brain." These scientists will have a really difficult time once they return to the other world. There is nothing that can be done. I believe all we can do is to put them in a "cocoon" that the materialistic people are often put into in the Spirit World. Then they will probably be left alone for several hundred years.

Unfortunately, people who are considered "excellent" in this world are often the ones who are misguiding this world. Although things that have recently developed may appear profound, we must know that the things that have been around for many years are not necessarily wrong. I do not reject medical science itself, but something very mysterious and spiritual is at the core of any illness. It can even be put like this: "Illnesses that were once curable have now become incurable because people in this world have lost belief in spirituality. Many illnesses have become incurable for this reason."

The physical body heals
When the spiritual body is restored

As I have mentioned earlier, pathological abnormalities first appear in the astral body, the outer most layer of the spiritual body, before lesions show up on the physical body. Part of the astral body is already ill and that part, which has becomes darkish, is where something alarming is taking place. Illnesses first appear on the spiritual body before they manifest on the physical body.

In trying to heal an illness, there is of course a way to cure it from the outside [physical body], but it is also possible to cure it from the inside [spiritual body]. Within the spiritual body, we have a part that is brightly shining as the child of God, the child of Buddha. If this inner light strongly wishes to heal the damaged part that has manifested on the outer most layer of the spiritual body, that damaged part will start to cure itself.

Once the spiritual body is completely healed, the physical body will also start to heal. This is something quite difficult, but when we return to the other world, there is no other way; we have to heal our spiritual body. In other words, the other world is the world where we can change our shape and form through our willpower. This is the true form of a human being. The physical body in this world is just like a shadow of that true from.

You may all probably think that the physical body is very solid and rigid, but in actual fact, this is not the case. The molecule that makes the physical body consists of atoms that are even smaller. If we observe the structure of the atom and if we exemplify the nucleus as a soccer placed in the middle of a soccer stadium, it will only look as if the electrons are moving in circles around the area of the stand. This is how hollow the physical body is. This kind of state has formed a type of magnetic field, making up a single atom. These atoms gather, making a molecule. The molecules then join together, creating the physical body.

Hence, the physical body is actually quite hollow. Our bodies are not solid and rigid; it is a gathering of very hollow entities conjoined together. Therefore, it can be said that the "building" will start to change if there is change in the "design."

Your physical body will change
In accordance with your mind

A number of worldly things can, of course, cause your body to fall ill. It could be physical causes, accidents or for other various reasons. However, in such cases, it is possible to overcome your physical ailments by changing your lifestyle on the basis of the rules of this world. For example, in terms of obesity, a person can easily lose weight by controlling what he eats and reducing his calorie intake. Alternatively, if one gets lung cancer by smoking too much, there is a high chance he can cure himself if he stops smoking.

Nonetheless, unless you discard the idea that human bodies are no different from cars, it becomes difficult to cure yourself through religious power however much you try. Our true form is, by all means, the spiritual body. Thus, our physical body changes in response to the spiritual body. Little by little, the state of the soul or the state of the mind permeates through to the outside and manifests on the outer appearance of a human being. In the same way, the spiritual body affects the condition of the physical body.

In the world after leaving this one, humans are in their true form and can freely change the way they want to look and are able to live a life full of creativity. Once people return to the other world, everyone will eventually learn how much they are able to freely change and transform their bodies. Likewise, in this world, people can change their appearance in accordance to their state of mind. This is similar to the teaching of T'ien-Tai Chih-i, who taught the theory of "one thought leads to three thousand worlds."

If an illness is caused by an unbalanced, unhealthy lifestyle, it would be as if you are trying to collect water in a bucket with many holes. If there is a clear cause and effect relationship between your health and your unbalanced or unhealthy lifestyle within the realm of this world, then you will need to accumulate small, diligent efforts in order to change yourself.

On the other hand, some may not care about their body in this world because essentially we are a completely spiritual being. However, there are certain rules in this world, so it is important not to become too reckless. Not everything that the doctors say is wrong. Things that they say are bad for the body, are usually so. However, it is when doctors say that an illness will *never* be cured that you must tell yourself, "That is not true. Humans can change their life by the way they think."

When you strongly wish for how you want to become, Things will move in that direction

As I mentioned in chapter one, there are two types of muscles—voluntary muscles that we can freely move the way we want and involuntary muscles, such as internal organs, that we cannot move the way we want. There may be rare people who are able to move their intestines the way they want, but involuntary muscles are usually known to be difficult to move. However, as long as involuntary muscles are part of the physical body, it is not true to say that they are completely out of our volition.

Metaphorically speaking, the difference between voluntary and involuntary muscle is similar to the difference between animals and plants. Animals move freely, while plants look motionless as if they are at a standstill. However, if you film a plant long enough and watch the video, you will see that it moves in various ways, such as growing and turning the flower or the leaves toward the sunlight. They grow wherever there is good supply of sunlight and water and move by their own convenience. In this way, by watching a filmed image of a plant at a high speed, you will notice that plants also move.

Similar to plants, although involuntary muscles are thought to have no freedom, in actual fact, they are slowly but surely changing with time. This does not only apply to involuntary muscles. The same goes for bones, including the skull and the inside of the brain. I believe many people are struggling because these do not move on their own accord, however, we should know that they do gradually change by training them toward a particular direction. The speed may vary, but if you strongly wish to become a certain way, in most cases you will be able to transform yourself toward that direction.

Human beings have this kind of power to create. This power can be exhibited for a good purpose or to bring about a bad cause to create something bad. In most cases, creation that works toward a bad direction is actually an illness. Generally, the underlying cause of an illness comes from an emotional breakdown. Additionally, if you have self-punishing thoughts or a strong sense of self-torment, that can gradually penetrate into your subconscious mind to create an illness. Please be careful of these things. If you realize that you have such thought within you, then you must start correcting it. Begin by correcting the thoughts.

3

Influences that *Ikiryo* and Stray Spirits Can Have on the Physical Body

Ikiryo *is a combination of a person's strong thought And his guardian spirit*

If you have strong hatred toward a certain person, there are times this hatred can make you ill. Conversely, you can also fall ill due to hatred or resentment from another person. We must be very careful with this. In regards to this, people in the Heian period [the Medieval period in Japan, 794-1185A.D.] surprisingly knew more about this than the people today.

People in the Heian period often used to call the *Onmyoji* [the yin-yang master], to cure their illnesses. In the literary works of that age, we often come across stories about an *Ikiryo* [evil spirits of living people] in possession. Even to this current day, however, from what I feel, I must say that Ikiryo does exist and such phenomena do exist.

The true identity of an Ikiryo is the person's guardian spirit, but there is more to it. The person's strong thought is combined with his guardian spirit. The guardian spirit and the person's own thought or, in other words, the thought of the person living in this world, combines together and powerfully approaches. If you have an attachment toward a particular person and have destructive thoughts or hatred such as, "I want to fire him," "I want to kick him away" or "I want him to die," then that thought will travel to the other person and firmly cling onto him. There are many cases where an illness starts to form on that particular person in this way.

For this reason, this clinging thought needs to be removed from the person. But back in the days, this was the job of Onmyojis. Therefore, the Onmyoji used to also play the role of a doctor. Such curses did actually take place and it seems, at the time, people use to return the curse to the curser.

Furthermore, politicians of the time used to use Onmyoji's strong willpower and the power of cursing to unseat their political enemy. Once one side realized that their opponent "hired" a person with strong willpower, they would fight back by "hiring" someone with even stronger willpower. In this way, I believe that period was very spiritual and their understanding on the power of thoughts was right and to the point, to some extent. People in the modern day are way too ignorant about the spiritual Truth. It is important that they study it.

Fundamentally, you can fight off most negative spirits, like Ikiryo, with *The Dharma of the Right Mind*, the fundamental sutra of Happy Science. It can mostly be removed by playing the CD in which I am reciting the prayers of this sutra book.

In addition, the practice of self-reflection that we teach at Happy Science is also very effective. There are cases in which various kind of matters from the past have accumulated in your mind like sludge. Thus, it is important to reflect on the past thoughts and actions to cleanse the mind. It is essential to gradually cleanse these matters by practicing self-reflection, by joining a ritual prayer of Happy Science and by various other practices. If the illness is caused by something from the inside, then effort must be made to remove this.

When you get possessed by a spirit that died Of an illness, the same symptoms will appear in you

Illnesses can be caused by physical factors, but it can also be caused by human relationships and various other thoughts. In addition, there a lot of illnesses that are caused by possession of evil spirits. In my books, I have written that such cases make up 70 or 80% of all the illnesses in general. We cannot clarify the degree since it is not possible to measure it statistically, but I believe around 70% of the cases are affected by a spiritual cause. If someone is possessed by a spirit of a person who died from an illness, the possessed person will have exactly the same symptoms.

For example, there are cases where an illness in a family is carried down from one generation to the next. From a medical perspective, this will probably be acknowledged as a genetic disease. Although it might be caused by a genetic disorder, we must also know that a deceased person may remain in their house as a stray spirit possessing the descendants, causing the same symptoms to manifest in the household.

In order to expel such spirits, we would fundamentally use the same method as we would use on the Ikiryo. If the mind of the person is corrected and lives with a well-refined mind, the evil spirits will leave the person. Of course, it is also possible to conduct a memorial service for the stray spirits.

This situation, in which the same symptoms of the spirit of the person who died of an illness manifesting on the person possessed, is something that I, myself, have witnessed from my own experience.

I have mentioned this in my book, *Cho Zettai Kenkoho* [The Way to Definite Health] (Tokyo: IRH Press, 2009), but my grandmother was a lady with strong willpower. She had eight children, but due to her foul mouth and selfish attitude, she spent her later years in the hospital since her children did not want to take care of her. Due to this reason, in trying to bring them toward her, she wrote the name of each child on a piece of paper as she whispered, "Come,

come," as though she recited a spell. Then she made a paper string out of them and tied it to the foot of her bed.

As the children started to get severe headaches, they visited the hospital assuming that it was their mother calling them. As expected, when they got there, the twisted paper with their name was tied on the bed-rail. My grandmother was probably a type of psychic.

A year after she passed away, or perhaps it was the year she died, the following event happened. When I returned home [Tokushima Prefecture] to attend the yearly *Obon* season [custom related to ancestral memorial], my mother suddenly started experiencing abnormalities in her body. She started to breathe heavily and as she broke out in a greasy sweat, she lay facing up, claiming that she had pain in her heart. It appeared as though she could die any minute.

Looking at the situation objectively, we would have needed to call an ambulance, but because it was the Obon season, I thought to myself, "Wait a minute. This is strange. Maybe some spirit is here" and decided to put some spiritual power in my mother. As I assumed, a possessing spirit appeared and that was my grandmother who passed away only recently. My grandmother's spirit said, "I am only able to return home during Obon season, because it is the only time the gates of Hell open. The gatekeeper takes a summer vacation and because he left, the gate of Hell just opened. I could come out of Hell and that is why I have returned." Then my mother started experiencing exactly the same symptoms my grandmother had before she passed away.

Since I understood the reason for my mother's abnormalities, I gave a short preach to my grandmother, recited "The Dharma of the Right Mind" and sent her back to the other world. She has now returned to Heaven, but she was in Hell at the time because it hadn't been long since she passed away. Although my mother was almost out of breath and everybody was about to call an ambulance, as soon as my grandmother's spirit dispelled, she calmly stood up and started working in the kitchen within five minutes. This change was so drastic that it would appear unbelievable.

Repelling evil spirit is possible Even from few hundred kilometers away

There was another similar incident that happened. I was in Tokyo at the time and my mother gave me a phone call and said, "I do not feel well. Maybe something is here again." Since I was unable to return to Tokushima Prefecture straight away, I decided to repel the evil spirit from Tokyo over the phone. It is also possible to do this. I asked my mother to hold on to the handset and said, "I will now begin to recite 'The Dharma of the Right Mind,' so please listen." As I repelled the evil spirit by reciting "The Dharma of the Right Mind," her symptoms completely disappeared after a while.

At the time of this event, since my father, Saburo Yoshikawa [Honorary Advisor of Happy Science] was still alive and well, I told him about this incident. But he scolded me and said, "It's as if I have no powers at all." It was probably something that I should have kept a secret from him. However, it was a surprise to me that we can repel evil spirits even when we are few hundred kilometers away. By repelling the evil spirit in this way, someone who was suffering moments before could walk up and down the stairs without any difficulty.

As just described, if a spirit of those who passed away with an illness comes to someone, in many cases the person will experience exactly the same symptoms as the spirit had when it was alive. Therefore, cancer centers or cancer wards are not desirable. There are a great number of dead spirits at such places and if you get possessed by one of them, there is a possibility that you will start having the same symptoms as the dead spirit. Therefore, it is doubtful whether such centers are actually good or not. It is fine to cure something that can be cured at the hospital, but it is not a good place to be for a long period of time. Once your health starts improving, it might be desirable to flee as soon as possible.

Almost all illness can be cured, but if one's duration of life is coming to an end, there is nothing much that can be done. You would become a nuisance if you live up to a thousand or two thousand years of age, so there will be a point where you will have to give up. It would be ideal if you could make sure that you remain alive at crucial times of your family. If you die during crucial times, it would make it easier for you to become a stray spirit. Therefore, it would be best if you could skillfully live through such times and receive a calling from the other world when the time comes.

4

Let's Cure Illnesses
With the Power of Faith

With strong thought, it is even possible
To shrink an enlarged heart

On July 2009, the Organ Transplantation Law was revised in Japan. Before this revision, children in Japan were unable to receive organ transplants and people had to collect tens of millions of yen of donations in order to fly to America where organ transplants could be held. However, the law was revised since people were desperate to get domestically recognized organ transplants from children who are declared brain-dead.

Nevertheless, since the patient is not exactly dead at the stage of brain death, it means that the law is justifying "legal murder" by this revision. The Japanese Diet is able to create laws for death penalty and in this way, the Diet has "the right to kill people." I guess it is fine to make such laws, but by enacting the law that connotes the meaning of considering those who are "about to die" as "dead," people who are against organ transplant become helpless.

An illness that considers a need for heart transplant is mainly an illness called "dilated cardiomyopathy."

This illness can be cured by shrinking the size of the heart to its normal size. The doctors think that an enlarged heart cannot return to its normal size since the knowledge that a heart is made up of pieces attached together like a cardboard or a cloth ball, is common practice for doctors. For this reason, the doctors believe that replacing it with another person's heart is the only way to treat the illness.

However, it is actually possible to shrink an enlarged heart. This may go against common medical practice, but there is no doubt that a heart can shrink. If anyone with faith experiences the same symptoms, I suggest you test it out. The heart will definitely shrink. You must hold a firm thought in shrinking it; tell your heart that it will get better by shrinking. Since the contractile force weakens if a heart enlarges, it makes the heart easier to function if it is smaller. Dilated cardiomyopathy is believed to be an incurable disease, but it can be cured in most cases.

An age in which the impossible becomes possible, Is approaching

However, there are illnesses that cannot be cured in spite of any effort. There are cases where it is necessary for us to die as our destiny. There are also cases in which becoming ill is part of life's plan. If this is the case, the illness may not be cured, but in general, I believe most illnesses can be cured.

There is no problem in treating a curable illness at a hospital, but the more incurable or rare the disease is, the higher the possibility that it is related to something spiritual. Therefore, I believe it is our turn when the doctors give up, saying that there is nothing they can do and that the illness cannot be cured at the hospital.

If an illness is incurable at a hospital, then please cure it through the power of faith. If you are a person suitable to be cured, it will be cured. By truly understanding the teachings of Happy Science, you will come to know that there is no way a disease cannot be cured.

Furthermore, since we have recently started drawing power from extraterrestrial beings, we have gone beyond the spiritual healing we had until now and have started the ritual prayers of "Pleiades Healing" and "Super Vega Healing."* An age when the impossible becomes possible is already here.

It may have become difficult for modern people to believe in such matters, but it is said that Jesus, who once died, had resurrected spiritually. Ophealis [a Great Guiding Spirit of Light, born in Greece several hundred years before 4,000 B.C. In the Egyptian mythology, He is known as Osiris.] is also known to have resurrected after his body was mutilated, by all the parts being put back together. These kinds of stories would make modern-day surgeons speechless, but according to my spiritual reading of extraterrestrial beings, Ophealis was resurrected by Vegans. By using the scientific technology of planets with advanced technology, I believe this is possible. Since we are currently drawing such power from extraterrestrial beings, more illnesses will be cured.

Aside from this, it is crucial that we create a better atmosphere of faith as a religious organization. By doing so, more and more miracles will occur. The DVDs of my lectures[*] also have an effect in treating illnesses, so please watch it as many times as you wish at the local branches and temples of Happy Science.

---

[*] For those who are interested in these ritual prayers or watching lecture DVDs, please refer to the contact information at the back of the book for your nearest branch.

Chapter Three

Ways to Make Cancer Vanish

Lecture given on October 24, 2010
at Yokohama Konandai Local Temple
Kanagawa, Japan

1
Curing Illnesses is
The Royal Road of Religion

Making cancer vanish is
The classic theme of religion

"Ways to Make Cancer Vanish" is the title of this chapter. This is an unusual topic for me to deal with and I have not talked much about it before, but it is a classic theme in the field of religion. Very few religious groups founded before World War II [WWII] went without mentioning, "Cancer can be cured." Rather, most of them tried to do missionary work on this theme. However, it has become somewhat difficult for religion to talk about it, due to the great advancements in modern medicine and hospitals after WWII.

Nonetheless, as we have often covered in our monthly magazine, *Happy Science Monthly*, we have seen many cases of cancer disappearing. I believe Happy Science should now earnestly state, as a religion, that illnesses are cured. Since many diseases have actually been proven to be cured, it is time we make a start on this theme.

Happy Science has been working on various activities such as the study of extraterrestrials, political activities and so on, but I believe that curing illnesses is another royal road of religion. It is about time for us to talk on this subject with confidence.

A man's ulcer disappeared
After a Q&A session with me

Last summer [2010], I gave a lecture at a local branch in Nagano Prefecture. After the lecture, there was a Q&A session and a man in his 50's asked me a question. [See the first question in Chapter 4.] He came to the branch with his father in his 80's and asked, "My father has lost most of his hearing because of an ear disorder. He does not listen to me no matter how hard I try to talk to him about the Buddha's Truth. What should I do for him?"

Upon hearing this, I conducted a spiritual reading on the spot and said, "You are responsible for your father's difficulty in hearing. He gradually lost his hearing because your uncompromising habits of lecturing him led him to strongly refuse to listen. It is because of you." I made a clear affirmation in front of a large audience that the cause of his father's disorder lay in him.

It must have been an unexpected answer for the son. He must have been surprised to be criticized, since he thought he was the one who had been making diligent effort in studying Buddha's Truth. He may have assumed that some kind of spiritual possession is causing his father's ear disorder and expected me to get rid of it. He might have believed that I would lecture his father by pointing out his mistakes.

However, it was he, not his father, who was scolded. He was told and pointed out, "It is you. You have a strong feeling of blame toward your parents. Unless you correct matters around that, your father's illness will not be cured. His unwillingness to listen to what you say has made him suffer from a hearing difficulty, so the problem lies within you." Although the son was surprised with my answer, he accepted it.

This was what happened during the lecture, but the story continued a few days later. This man, in actual fact, had a medical checkup the previous month and was found to have a rectal ulcer of about 10 centimeters in diameter. However, after I scolded him and he began to thoroughly reflect on himself, his ulcer completely disappeared by the time of his reexamination. It took the doctor by surprise. I did not give him guidance in order to heal his disease; I just pointed out that it is his fault and that his attitude toward his father was wrong.

However, what I told him was something he never imagined. He realized that the problem laid in him and did self-reflection. He brought his father to the local branch of Happy Science, assuming that his father is the one who is wrong and to make his father accumulate virtues; however, he himself was scolded instead. After returning home, he started to reflect on himself and his ulcer completely disappeared. The spiritual healing worked on the son who asked the question, not his father who had the hearing problem. Instead of his father's hearing loss, his own ulcer was cured.

This is what really happened in a certain power spot in Nagano. This did not happen long ago. It happened just recently [2010]. I never attempted to cure the disease. I just pointed out the mistakes he made in his thoughts and scolded him to change his mind. But as a result, his ulcer disappeared and his illness was cured. This kind of thing does happen.

Illnesses can often be cured
When we realize the causes we were not aware of

Human beings are often unaware of the mistakes in their own thoughts. It is difficult to look at ourselves objectively, so people often misunderstand and try to find reasons to their problems in factors outside of them. Illness is a typical example.

However, common diseases such as colds are caused by physical factors. If you walk outside wearing light clothing in midwinter, you will most likely catch a cold. This is not surprising. Unlike such common illnesses, some serious incurable diseases are caused by psychological problems. In fact, in many cases, illnesses are caused by thoughts that you unknowingly hold. The unseen problem that is below the surface of your mind develops itself over a long period of time and progresses into a disease.

Among the books that I have written, there is a book that focuses on the theme of curing illnesses, called *Cho Zettai Kenkoho* [The Way to Definite Health] (Tokyo: IRH Press, 2009). One of my secretaries gave this book to her grandfather. Although he does not usually read any of Happy Science books, he read this particular one for some reason and his dementia, in other words his senility he was suffering from, was medically cured by merely reading this book. This happened to a person close to me; therefore, it is highly credible. Since her grandfather is still alive, there is strong evidence.

As this case shows, dementia can be cured by simply reading a Happy Science book. Thus it shows there are various ways as to which illnesses can be cured in what way. In most cases, because people are unaware of the cause of their illnesses, there is a strong tendency for an illness to be cured when the person finds out the reason himself.

There are parts of our mind that we are unaware of. If it is those parts that are causing the illness, the disease will begin to break away and be cured when you come to realize them through the guiding light of the Buddha's Truth.

After all, spiritual existence is the essence of human beings and the spiritual existence that dwells in the physical body influences it. In fact, the spirit body is the "master" while the physical body is the "subordinate."

Ultimately, as it is stated in one of the fundamental sutras of Happy Science called, "Words of Truth: The Dharma of the Right Mind" in *Buddha's Teaching: The Dharma of the Right Mind*, "The physical body is the shadow of the soul." If you shift your state of your mind to this perspective, changes will begin to appear in your physical body.

Nonetheless, in respect to what part of your mind is wrong and distorted, you will need to discover this yourself by studying the Buddha's Truth and through conversations with your Dharma friends.

Unless you establish faith,
It is difficult to cure diseases through religion

Aside from the mild diseases that are commonly known, I believe about 70 percent of the severe diseases that affect our lives can even be cured to some extent. Since we have experienced a number of such cases at Happy Science, I am thinking it is about time to systemize the methods for curing them.

There is a reason as to why I have not taught about "healing illnesses" until now. It is because, in the end, it is difficult for religion to cure illnesses unless there is established faith. Therefore, it is firstly important to consider whether one has established faith.

In the New Testament, Jesus repeatedly said, "Do you believe that I am able to do this?" He asked people if they had faith and said, "It shall be done to you according to your faith." Illnesses cannot be cured without an established faith. This is because not being able to have established faith proves the unwillingness to believe in something that is not of this world and of greater power beyond this world.

If we only look at things from the perspective of this world, there is so little we can do. Modern medical science observes the human body based on materialism and tends to treat it the same way as we would treat a car that has broken-down.

Nonetheless, the human body has the power to heal illnesses. There are various methods and tools we use to treat illnesses, such as surgery and medication. However, those things, by themselves, are not enough. People originally possess the ability to heal themselves, so the illness can be cured.

It is a superstition that illnesses can be cured through surgery alone. An operation involves cutting open the body and it is very much like committing *hara-kiri* [committing suicide by disembowelment] in olden Japan. Even though this procedure is hurting the bodies and putting lives at risk due to loss of blood, in a sense, the belief that operations can cure illnesses leads to healing.

Doctors believe that removal of the diseased areas can cure illnesses, but being able to create the disease means the power to produce them is originally inherent in the human body. Hence, even if the affected area is removed by surgery, one can create the same one in another part of the body if they wish to. This is known as "metastasis." For this reason, it is necessary to cure the source of it.

2

Why are there People Who Get Cancer?

Even good people can get cancer

There are so many diseases that it is quite difficult to explain each individual case. So in this chapter, I would like to focus on cancer.

Although I have already mentioned in my book, *The Way to Definite Health* [as already cited], I would like to mention the following once again, just in case— "bad people get cancer, but good people do not" is not necessarily true. Even those who worked hard and did great job often die from cancer. But if others consider them to be bad people, they would probably feel disappointed and be unable to return to Heaven.

People do not get cancer because they are bad. Cancer is one of the major causes of death and is simply another form of death. Many people die of cancer, but that does not mean they are all evil. Nevertheless, when you get cancer, there seems to be a certain rule. If the rule is set in motion, even good people can develop cancer and die from it.

These people are usually the ones who have a strong sense of responsibility. They take on demanding tasks, feel a lot of pressure and often undergo suffering, distress and mental conflicts. These suffering, distress and mental stress materialize and manifest themselves as illnesses. During such times, there are various ailments that can appear on the body and one of the typical phenomena is cancer.

A foreign object that forms inside the body is a tumor And one that forms outside the body is a wart

In the case of cancer, a foreign object that should not exist according to the blueprint of the human body starts to grow. They take form in the internal organ. First, a tumors forms and that tumor grows into cancer cells. When the cancer cell enlarges and spreads around the body, the person is told by the doctor, "Your cancer has metastasized. We can no longer cure it. It is too late," and the person eventually dies.

However, it is a tumor only when such foreign object develops inside the body. If it develops outside the body, it is just a wart. Therefore, having a tumor develop inside the body is actually the same thing as having a wart develop on the outside of the body.

Many of you may have experienced having a wart before. Around 1990, I, myself, had a wart at the lower part of my left cheek when I gained some weight, but when I lost weight, it disappeared. It is as simple as that. In short, it was just excess fat and bodily waste that appeared on the outside of the body. I do not have it now. It has completely disappeared.

Likewise, when you have a wart on the internal organs, it is called a tumor. A wart is something unnecessary for the body and it is like toxin that the body wants to excrete and get rid of. Toxin becomes a wart when it is squeezed out of the body and is materialized. When that wart appears outside of the body, it can be healed by applying various types of medications. However, when it grows inside of the body, it sounds more serious that an operation may become necessary.

For example, from my junior or senior year in high school until a short while after I entered university, I often had warts on my hands. But I have never developed one ever since except for the case I mentioned earlier. At that time, Job's tears was said to be good for warts. I was advised to take a decoction of Job's tears, a kind of plant, and apply the dregs onto the wart, so I tried it. I am not sure if it was effective, but my wart certainly disappeared before I knew it, so it probably did work.

Looking back, I may have been under a lot of stress at the time, preparing for my university entrance exams. Therefore, I ate a lot to boost my stamina, resulting in weight gain. However, after I entered university, PE class started and I also began spending less on food in order to buy books. Then, when I realized, I had lost seven to eight kilograms in a single semester. I have not developed a wart ever since, so warts may simply be caused by weight gain.

The same goes for foreign objects that form on the internal organs. The desire to excrete something toxic may ultimately be creating such lesions. Such lesions do not necessarily have to be recognized as cancer. If such toxins are excreted from the body in a different way, it will not necessarily be cancer.

The self-destructive desire in the subconscious Causes cancer

I have mentioned the psychological tendency of those who are likely to get cancer. I also gave words of reassurance that those who are prone to getting it are not necessarily bad people. However, I would like to point out that holding in too much anger will make it prone for people to get cancer. When one loses his temper and holds it in for too long, they are likely to get cancer. There is such tendency.

On the other hand, people who take their anger out directly often earn frowns by those around. In this case, they themselves do not fall ill but will make others sick instead. In addition, mental breakdowns such as failing an exam or in business, falling out of love and getting into an accident can also cause illness. When people experience these types of mental breakdowns, they unknowingly try to become ill and look for any part of the body that is vulnerable to a disease, resulting in some illness manifesting itself on the area.

If people have a physical predisposition that easily develops cancer, the disease will manifest itself as cancer. It can also appear as vascular or brain disease. There are even people who create quite strange unknown disease.

In the case of cancer, it is usually triggered by being confronted with distress through some unfavorable incident in life and the desire for self-destruction grows and progresses on a subconscious level.

Happy Science has been holding "Prevention against suicide campaigns," but we actually must wage such a campaign for ourselves. Sometimes we could be unknowingly holding "suicide promotion campaign" in ourselves. When we make a big mistake, there may be times when we feel like we want to die of embarrassment. Such feelings create illnesses.

However, even if one may think he is in serious trouble and in pain, it often may not seem like a big deal from the eyes of others. As the saying "lookers-on see more than the players" goes, when others see it far from the outside, it is often the case that the matter all seems common and usual.

Suppose a company is in serious management trouble and on the blink of bankruptcy. It may be a cataclysmic event for the president of the company. However, in reality, nearly 20,000 companies in Japan go bankrupt every year, so it is not too unusual that a company gets into serious management problems when times are tough in the industry and go bankrupt as a result. However, if the president treats the failure of his company as something that should not happen and is over shocked by it, he will most likely fall ill.

By getting sick, he may be able to avoid responsibility before the company goes broke and can attribute the failure of his business to his poor physical condition. Even if the company goes bankrupt, he can even evade responsibility by saying, "My company was not meant to collapse, but it broke down due to my sickness."

Thus, when the company runs into financial difficulties, the president begins to destroy his body. Consciously, he does not think about destroying his body, but deep down in his subconscious mind, he actually tries to do so in order to protect his pride. If a person refuses to make a mistake, such kind of thing happens.

Those who are likely to get breast cancer
Or uterus cancer

The same goes for the issues between men and women. Poor marital relationship can often cause cancer. Women are highly likely to develop breast or uterus cancer. Holding in inner conflict caused by marital quarrels and accumulating the negative thoughts for a long period causes cancer to appear in the area of the body peculiar to women.

It is not a matter of good or bad. It is common that we are sometimes unable to adjust ourselves with our relationships with others and be caused to struggle and worry. Stresses like this appear in various parts of the body.

In recent years, the number of single women who get breast cancer have been increasing. This may also have to do with inner conflict. Struggling with the conflict between the desire to get married and have children and the desire to work and keep a job often makes it prone for breast cancer to develop. This is because such illness creates an opportunity for these people to give up the hope of getting married. This kind of thing happens when the hope to concentrate on their career is strong.

Additionally, in the case of uterine disease, marital problems and conflicts between parents and children can often be the cause. However, prior to the disease, there must be some retaliation of anger between husband and wife or parents and children. There probably is an incredible amount of dissatisfaction that has built up over time.

3

A Mental Attitude to Fight Illnesses

Illnesses also serve the role of Protecting one's pride

In a sense, illness is an SOS directed to oneself. It is a warning signal from the body. In another sense, it is clearly explaining the mistakes one had made in this world and plays a role of protecting oneself from it. An illness is actually trying to protect one's pride. If people lose their pride, they will lose the will to live.

If one refuses to acknowledge the fact that things did not go well in his work or his personal relationships because of his own lack of ability and talent, his body will try to speak those feelings instead. As a consequence, an illness can naturally appear. This is because an illness can allow people to make excuses to say, "I originally wanted to do so and so, but now I cannot because of my illness." Therefore, if your illness is caused by inner conflict, it can be cured when you decide to hereafter change your mind completely on a certain day.

This even holds true for atopic dermatitis. For example, it is often reported that when the mother with a child, who suffers from atopic dermatitis, awakens to the Truth and changes her mind, the atopic skin sloughs off from the child's face and a smooth skin reveals itself.

After all, the problems we have in our mind are expressed on to the body. The mind is like an artist. As if an artist drawing a picture on a white canvas, it expresses its will on the body. Human beings, so to speak, have a mind that we are "aware of" and a mind that we are "not aware of." The mind that we are not aware of is the one that it informing us of our situation through lesions and illnesses. We need to observe our situation objectively. If we become ill or experience poor physical condition, please try and look back and think if there were incidents that happened prior to the illness.

My experience of temporarily getting farsightedness Due to stress from children's education

My vision is now 20/12 without glasses and I can see very well. I am embarrassed to tell this, but roughly 10 years ago when I was 44, my vision deteriorated and I could not read very well. So I bought a lot of reading glasses and placed them all around my house. I also hung a strap around my neck and attached it to a pair of glasses as I moved around the house.

At the time, I thought, "I guess I'm growing old, my eyes are getting weak. I had such good eyesight..."

However, when I thought about it carefully, I began to feel that it may have something to do with my child's entrance examination. I realized that my vision weakened due to the stress from it. It was just before my first child took the entrance examination and I, myself, had suffered the strain of worry. As I thought that this situation was the cause of my weakened vision, I decided to put my reading glasses away to see if I could read without them. In a week or so, my eyesight returned back to normal. If I had kept wearing the glasses, I would probably still have bad eyesight.

I can still read about 2,000 books a year without glasses. Furthermore, I can do so even in a posture that would usually strain my eyes. The reason I can do this is because I always remind my eyes with a determined mind that "I have to read books" and that "my eyes are a business tool, so it will be a problem for me if my eyes go bad."

When we experience psychological shock, we often say things like "I cannot see the light at the end of the tunnel." Indeed, this phrase fits perfectly. If we feel that our future is totally bleak, we can really lose our eyesight.

To some extent, accept the things
That we cannot control

There was a time I got calculus in my body. When I carefully checked the dates I got them, I found that they often formed when my children took the nation-wide trial exams. The date of the trial exams coincided perfectly with the time when I got stones, with 100 percent accuracy. It did not happen at the time of the minor exams but at the time of the major exams. It made me realize I must have suffered from a lot of mental strain.

When my first child faced the entrance examination, I was not used to the whole process. But I became accustomed to it as my second and third children went through theirs. When I looked through the results of the test, I was able to advise them by saying, "You cannot rely on these trial exams. People with a pass rate of 80 percent could fail, while those with 20 or even 5 percent could pass, so no one knows what will happen until you really take the actual exam."

If children also change the way they think and recognize that it is acceptable to be happy if they pass the exam and be disappointed if they fail and to humbly accept the result and keep refining to the fullest, they wouldn't have to experience so much shock. As a matter of fact, to reach such a level will require spiritual discipline in this world.

I just used children as an example, but the same holds true for adults as well. There must be a great number of times when you felt disgusted with yourself for making mistakes in your job. In addition, there are probably situations where you are blamed by others in reality. When this happens, illnesses would be created immediately. This may sound harsh, but people actually create their own illness. Then, as soon as someone falls ill, people stop accusing the person in an instant. Thus a great number of illnesses are self-created.

This is especially true as people grow old. Since they often find themselves less helpful to others when they are old, they begin to want an illness as an excuse. In order to defend themselves from being blamed by those around them, an illness starts to form. However, once they are ill, they tend to moan and groan to others from losing control of their own body.

So this is what I think. This world is not very much liberated and we cannot control everything. There are many things that do not work out the way we want them to. Therefore, I believe it is better to accept this fact to some extent.

After all, not everybody is able to enter the school or the company of their first choice or win the one million dollar lottery. If everyone won the one million dollar lottery, the lottery association would certainly go bankrupt. The same goes for *pachinko*, or Japanese pinball. If every ball scores a jackpot, the pachinko parlor would certainly go out of business. The machines are set, so that only 25 percent of the balls enter the target holes.

In this manner, this world is made in a way that things will not necessarily go our way. But at the same time, this is what gives life depth and meaning.

Overcome life's difficulties
With the strength of the mind

Many incidents happen in the course of our lives and they give rise to all kinds of distress. We face various difficulties, but how we overcome them is what is important. Just like a surfer catching the waves, we must ride out difficulties the best we can so that we do not suffer serious damage by it. It is when we fail and become beaten like a capsized yacht that we become seriously ill. Whether or not we can ride out difficulties could be related to the strength of our mind.

Last year, I published the book entitled, *Sutorongu Maindo* [Strong Mind] (Tokyo: IRH Press, 2010), but it is important to overcome difficult situations with such a strong mindset. If we have a weak mind, we will suffer tremendous damage over small incidents that ordinary people can easily cope with. The incident may even start to look like a huge problem if it is remembered over and over in the mind.

At such times, in a sense, people would be constantly thinking about themselves and their way of thinking would become self-centered. From the eyes of others, this is easy to see; but the person himself is not aware of it and would be imagining that he is in big trouble.

However, just like the waves, we must ride them out. It is important that we promptly overcome them and steer our life in a positive and constructive direction. We must have the strength to successfully ride out the wave of difficulties.

4

How to Make Cancer Vanish

Life has ups and downs

After all, what is it that we should do to make cancer vanish? Most cancers are caused by inner suffering and conflicts triggered by tangled personal relationships. In life, like a difficult jigsaw puzzle, there are probably a large number of problems that may seem impossible to solve. If we struggle with such problems, cancer is highly likely to form.

Of course, there may be problems that cannot be solved right away. But in this world, even though the problem cannot be solved right this moment, there are many problems that can be solved over time. This is something we must accept as a fact and be determined to endure it.

An old Japanese statesman Kaishu Katsu [1823 – 1899], who played an active role around the time of the Meiji Restoration, advocated the theory of the "10-year cycle" of life. He said that life changes with the cycle of every 10 years or so. Indeed, life does consist of ups and downs during a period of about 10 years. When times are good, we may get treated well and may even get a promotion; however, once times start going downhill, we have to remain in a slump for about 10 years. Nonetheless, we should not be too discouraged during our unfavorable times nor should we overreact. Rather, it is important that we use that time to build inner strength to prepare for the next ten years of upturn.

Although Kaishu Katsu was living amid such chaotic age and was attempted by assassins more than 20 times, he fulfilled his life until the age of 77. This is probably equivalent of living up to around the age of 100 in present time. He died right after he got out of bath one day. After he took a few steps in the hallway, he felt something got to his heart and died on the spot. Unlike many other samurai leaders of the Restoration period who were murdered, I believe he lived his life very skillfully, since he lived to such age and died peacefully.

A person of such character said that life has a cycle. Therefore, it is important that every one of you take an elevated view of life to some extent and accept the fact that life has good times as well as bad times.

Preparing ourselves for the worst

Life will not constantly bring favorable winds and may not be full of good fortunes or successes in life. But please ride out the adversities skillfully. I am sure you have received various "poisons" from others. But since it is their choice to let out poison, there is nothing that can be done. However, you must make sure that you do not get affected too much. There are many people who throw "poisonous balls" in this world and it cannot be helped. It will require a tremendous amount of energy to stop them from doing so. Nonetheless, you do not have to be affected by them. Of course, it is difficult to stay completely unaffected by all the negativities, but we must learn to let them go even if we receive them and to not give them so much heed.

"All things are impermanent" in this world, so change your mind so that it becomes like the clear water flowing down the stream. Please try not to make the problems bigger than they actually are. Additionally, life is made so that you can somehow get through by preparing yourself to accept the worst possible scenario. What would be the worst scenario for people with cancer? That would be death.

However, I have already published books that explain in detail about life after death. The "destination map" already exists. If you read those books, you will learn everything about the world after death. There is nothing to worry about. Those who are unaware of what will happen after death will probably suffer when the time of death approaches. But we already have a good knowledge on it. We already know about it. Happy Science has clearly explained matters that have not been proven in the field of medicine, such as about the world after death.

In addition, there is still time for preparation even if the time of death is surely approaching. If you were to consider this period of three months, six months or even a year as the days left until your "entrance exam for the other world," you should spend the time on studying. If you can raise your life's score in this world, you will be able to return to the other world happily. Those who have very little days to live must give their best before their lives end. Cancer may lead you to death, but everyone dies in the end.

No one can live eternally. So, if you find that your time here on earth is nearly up, accept the reality and work hard to spend the rest of your life in the way that will add to your scores of this lifetime.

Simple methods to deal with cancer

1) First, hold gratitude in your mind

Now, I would like to teach you a few simple ways to deal with cancer. First, have gratitude in your heart. Those who have cancer often lack the heart of gratitude. People who are not very grateful toward their parents appear to be prone on developing cancer. They are not aware of it themselves, but they take what the parents have done for granted and show very little gratitude. Therefore, if you get cancer, you must hold gratitude toward your parents. You must also hold gratitude toward your family, friends, acquaintances, Dharma friends and various people around you. This is one of the important points.

2) *Reflect on the past incidents to the extent you are responsible for*

Another important point is to properly reflect on the past to the extent you are responsible for. There may be problems that are beyond your responsibility. For example, even if you regret that you couldn't take responsibility for the Great Depression, it is beyond the capacity of ordinary people and the blame does not lie in you. It is rather to be considered by the central bank governor or the World Bank. You cannot take responsibility to such extent, but please reflect on your past within the range of your own responsibility.

3) *Try to restore personal relationships and pray for the other person's happiness*

As for personal relationships, it is important to restore the ones that can be restored. As for relationships that are not possible to mend, please pray in your mind. For example, you can apologize in your mind by saying, "Ms./Mr. XXX, I am sorry for all my carelessness and when I went too far and hurt you. I am really sorry." Or, pray for the person's happiness. In this way, please practice gratitude, self-reflection and prayer.

4) Make an effort to smile

Lastly, train yourself to smile as much as possible. A smile can cure cancer, so try to have a smile on your face. Smile is a "magic bullet" for treating cancer. As people grow old, they often find it difficult to keep smiling. But the less they smile, the more likely they fall ill. Therefore, please practice smiling.

A smile is an expression of love toward others. Elderly people with pleasant smiles are loved. It is very simple. They are loved not because they have money. If they have money to offer to their grandchildren as pocket money, they will certainly be loved. But even without money, elderly people who always have a smile on their face are generally loved. A smile costs nothing. If you become an elderly person with a pleasant smile, you will be loved by others and if you are loved, that love will serve as a therapeutic medicine that gives you the power to relieve your worries and cure your illness.

So, please make an effort to put on a smile as part of your therapeutic medication. A smile only takes a bit of mental effort and habitual practice. Give love to others with a smile. It is just like a sunflower. A sunflower opens itself widely toward the sun and is always facing the sun. This is what a sunflower does. In life, there will be various happenings with distress and sufferings, but we should face toward happiness and smile as much as we can. Appreciate what you already have. Rather than focusing on what you don't have, give thanks to what you are already given.

In this way, practice of gratitude centered on your parents and self-reflection are what are generally needed. In addition, restore any human relationships that you can. If that is not possible, apologize to them in your mind through prayer. Lastly, always make an effort to smile as a remedy. Please use these methods to fight cancer. It may be hard to believe, but they are actually more effective than the medications prescribed at hospitals. It doesn't cost a penny, so please take my words openheartedly and give them a try. It will work.

The most effective medicine is faith

Of course, please acknowledge that the most effective remedy is faith. Many illnesses have been cured even at other religions besides Happy Science. More so at Happy Science; many more illnesses are supposed to be cured since our religion receives guidance from El Cantare. Faith is a form of culture in religion. Hence, the more the power of belief of our followers strengthens, the more greater number of diseases will be cured. Various kinds of illnesses will be cured. The number of cases is still not enough. As our followers' faith becomes stronger, we will be able to cure a hundred times as many diseases than we do now.

As the most powerful remedy, I sincerely pray that all of you will establish faith. Please believe that there is no disease that cannot be cured.

Chapter Four

Spiritual Readings of Diseases – Q&A Sessions

Question 1
Lecture given on August 11, 2010
at Ueda Local Temple
Nagano, Japan

Question 2 - 4
Lecture given on October 24, 2010
at Yokohama Konandai Local Temple
Kanagawa, Japan

1
The Causes of Ear Cancer and Cerebral Infarction

QUESTIONER 1:

I would like to ask some questions about a disease that my father has. He is currently 82 years old. When he was 40 years old, he was afflicted with ear cancer [pearl tumor] and today, he can barely hear anything. In addition, not only did he undergo surgery for bowel cancer when he was in his 60s, but he also recently fell ill of cancer in the esophagus.

RYUHO OKAWA:

It sounds as many as "department store of diseases."

Q1:

Yes. Even though my father has faith, no matter how much I try to convey to him Buddha's Truth, he does not listen to a word I say. While we were on our way to the lecture today, I told my father, "Since you will not be able to hear the lecture, try and feel Master's words with your heart." I wonder why my father gets cancer one after the other... so many times.

OKAWA:

Yes, too many times.

Q1:

But my father is very dedicated to life and is very energetic. Hence, I think he has some sort of mission. What can I do to awaken my father to this faith?

OKAWA:

Firstly, we should look into why your father has been getting cancer. Shall we take a look spiritually?

Q1:

Thank you very much.

The father's illness is caused by the conflict Between parent and child

OKAWA:

What is your father's name?

Q1:

His name is xxx.

OKAWA:

The person sitting next to you must be him.

Q1:
Yes.

OKAWA:
OK. Please give me some time.
[*He holds out his right hand at the podium and starts the spiritual reading. About 5 seconds of silence.*]

Why does this person get cancer so many times?
[*About 15 seconds of silence.*]

Hmm.
[*About 15 seconds of silence.*]

The cause lies in you [*pointing to the questioner*]. Yes.

Q1:
I'm sorry.

OKAWA:
The cause is you. You are the cause.
[*About 5 seconds of silence.*]

There are two reasons.
[*About 5 seconds of silence.*]

First, there is a lot of conflict. There must have been a conflict with your father in the past. What is this conflict?
[*Three seconds of silence.*]

Both of you seem to be excellent people. The conflict arose because both of you are competing on who is better than the other? I can hear you saying in your heart, "Be quiet, Dad! I am better than you, so just keep quiet!" I have a feeling this "be quiet, Dad!" is causing the cancer in your father's ear.

So I think your father's illnesses are caused by this conflict between parent and child. While you are trying to save your father, you are actually carrying this conflict with him inside you. This is one of the reasons for the illness.

You must not compete with your father. You must shift your mind toward saving other people around the world. You can have gratitude to your father, but he is not someone you are to compete against, so you must not get into a conflict with him.

Hampered childhood dream

There is one more. The other main reason is...
[*About 10 seconds of silence.*]

It lies in your childhood.
[*About 5 seconds of silence.*]

Well, I guess this also has to do with a conflict between parent and child, but I am thinking that when you were a child, your father told you not to do something you really wished to do. Do you remember something like that happening?

Q1:

I think I was allowed to do everything that I wished to do... so I can't think of anything in particular.

OKAWA:

Hmm. Is that so? This happened before you could walk or talk, when you were really young. Even if you have already forgotten it, if you take the time to reflect on yourself by breaking your life into segments from when you were born up until now, I assure you that you will remember.

There was something you truly wished to do, but your parents stopped you from doing it and I think you felt very unsatisfied. It can be assumed that you became very frustrated with your parents at the time. You have probably forgotten it by now. However, if you reflect on your past you will recall this incident. These are the two points.

The person who is causing your father's cancer is you. Since you are the reason, you should not think about standing above your father too much. If you do, it will create many illnesses. Your father is creating many illnesses in order to resist and annoy you.

Characteristics typical to people who get strokes

Q1:
I, myself, had a stroke about three months ago.

OKAWA:
I see. In many cases, people who get cerebral infarctions are generally very short-tempered and tend to be hysteric. They become angry very quickly. In order to prevent yourself from getting a stroke, it is important that you maintain a peaceful mind. You need to avoid that extra blood rush to your head by making an effort to bring the blood down to your *tanden* [by the abdomen, located below your belly button]. When you calm down and become a tolerant person, you will start to become stable and less angry over small things.

I think you should allow your father more freedom. He has lived up to the age of 82, so I think he should live the rest of his life the way he wants to. There is no need for you to control him. There are many other people who are waiting for your help. I think it is better for you to help them instead. There is a conflict between the family members in the background. I could explain on this further, but since we have the public audience and this Q&A session is being recorded, I will refrain from it.

Psychic powers are actually very "scary." Although I can explain what is happening in much finer details, within them there are things I should not say, which is also why I will keep it abstract.

If you practice self-reflection, I am sure a number of things will surface.

2

How to Consider Kidney Disease And Loss of Vision

QUESTIONER 2:

I am currently in my 60s. Since I started my own company at the age of 25, I have walked a career path as a manager of my company. Around the time I started my business, I was hospitalized for about nine months and a half with a kidney disease.

Two years ago, the doctor at the hospital told me that my kidney disease is getting worse and that it has reached the level of a renal failure. Now as I fight this disease, I'm strongly wishing to somehow complete the work that I am doing now. Please offer me advice on the kind of attitude I should keep.

Spiritual reading on
The "consciousness of the kidney" of the questioner

OKAWA:

OK. Can you stay standing for me?

[*He holds out both hands from the podium in the direction of the questioner's stomach standing in the front row. About 5 seconds of silence. He takes away his right hand and keeps his left hand held out.*]

Hmm, I am talking with the consciousness of your kidney right now. I am asking your kidney.
[*About 5 seconds of silence.*]

Your kidney is telling me that you overwork yourself. It is saying, "Because this person overworks himself, the burden is very heavy."

You seem to be a hard worker. Ever since you started your company, you have pushed yourself very hard. Since your work hours are very long with a lot of stress and you need to meet with a lot of people, your intake of tea and water is much higher than in general.

Q2:
Yes. Yes, that is true.

OKAWA:
You probably drink twice the amount compared to an average person.

Q2:
Yes.

OKAWA:
Perhaps you drink more than that. You drink two or three times more tea, coffee or black tea than the average person.

Your kidneys are extremely overworked and it is tired. Your kidney is saying, "I am working far beyond the capacity of a normal kidney. The extreme intake of liquid is caused by stress from work. Therefore you rely on drinks for comfort. So you need to get rid of the stress."

I am speaking in place of your kidneys. Kidneys have its own consciousness, but I am speaking for it since I feel pity that it doesn't have a mouth to speak for itself. "I understand the need for comfort and it is fine that you drink for refreshment. However, there is too much liquid intake, so please, perhaps, use a smaller cup.

You can drink as many times as you like, but please decrease the amount that you take in at once. And please make more time for exercise and physical work, so there is more chance for the body to perspire." This is what your kidneys are saying. I am not aware of your situation in detail, but your kidneys are saying that it has overworked for a number of years.

Business managers generally have some sort of stress and it usually manifests into illnesses or diseases in some part of the body. This is what is called "the president illness." When there is too much liquid intake, it often appears in either your kidneys or your heart. Too much liquid intake will cause kidneys to be overburdened and fall ill.

Alternatively, it will increase the amount of blood in the body, overburden the heart to pump more blood around the body and cause high blood pressure. Eventually, when your blood vessels start weakening, they will be overburdened then and will explode. In this way, people tend to get a disease in either their kidney or their heart.

Although you seem to be a hard worker, your kidney's opinion is that it is overburdened, so you need to take away some of that burden.

Set your order of priority in work
And delegate work to other people

You need to find other ways to reduce your stress besides liquid intake. This is basic of the basics in management, but one of the ways is to return to the starting point and set the order of priority in your work. In other words, you need to prioritize what you must do and start on your important work first. If there is something that is lower down your priority list that doesn't require your attention, you should assign it to other people and leave it up to them. This is one way of thinking.

Another way is to make posteriority, in other words to make a list of subordinates. It means to make a list of what you do not need to do and leave that work to other people or do it another day when you have more time.

In other words, you need to organize and narrow down your work, so that it becomes less of a workload. In management, taking initiative and setting good examples for others come first and it is a matter of course. Otherwise, no one will follow you. However, in the end, business should be managed through and with people. It cannot be done on your own.

Of course, if the president takes initiatives and sets good examples for others, the employees will follow the president and that will make a good start for the company. However, this cannot continue on to the end. There has to be a gradual shift toward allowing your company to progress through the power of people.

For example, Eiichi Shibusawa managed 500 to 600 companies. This is an extraordinary number. When it comes to managing such a number of companies, there is no way one can manage them decently. He must have had the knack for management and made sure he covered the crucial points in running his companies. Moreover, he must have had the skill to daringly appoint people and use their skills.

You need to listen to your kidneys request and return to the principle of management. Business should be thrived through its people. If you reorganize your priorities and so forth, you should be able to work for much longer. There are ways to work without overburdening yourself. It is not desirable for you to have the attitude toward work thinking, "I'll work vigorously until I die." You need to decrease your load and learn to relax.

I also have the tendency to overwork myself, so I might not be in the position to talk about this subject, but these are the two points that I wish to bring to your attention. I think you will be able to overcome your situation if you pay attention to these two points.

When one function weakens, Another function may develop over time

This is what I can say about your kidney, but do you have any other problem apart from your kidney?

Q2:
I am already 66 years old, so my eyesight is getting worse. It is actually becoming difficult for me to read books...

OKAWA:
Your eyes are fine as they are. We try to ensure all Happy Science books are printed in large prints. Today's lecture [Chapter 3 of this book] will be published as a book and we will make every effort to print it with large prints, so that it is easy to read. If you are at the age of 66, it is enough that you are able to see. There are actually a lot

of people who have accomplished great things even if they lost their eyesight.

I travel all over Japan to give lectures and, when I do, I usually get a massage the day before the lecture, at the hotel I stay. I must say that massagers are very intelligent people. One time there was a massager who told me that he had given me a massage 10 years ago. It was unbelievable. He also told me that my weight dropped by "x" kilograms since then and it was true. His memory is this good because his hands remember. The memories are not in his brain, but in his hands.

In addition, massagers also remember their clients' voice very well. One of them told me, "I heard this voice last November. I think I gave you a massage then." I was very surprised as I had him massage me at a different hotel at that time. So some people can remember with their hands and their ears even if they have lost their eyesight.

When humans lose an ability of any function, a different function can start to develop. There is still hope for our bodies. If your eyesight gets worse, just think that some other part will get better and improve. When you believe that "other functions such as my ears, my mouth or my head will improve its function to cover up for my loss of eyesight," an alternative function will start to develop without a doubt.

If you continue to train yourself, your abilities will develop even if you are 70 or 80 years old. Do not worry, as long as you do not lose your aspiration, your abilities will improve. I look forward for your further accomplishments.

3

Reasons behind Ovarian Resection, Breast Cancer and Brain Tumor

QUESTIONER 3:

I would like to ask a question about my mother's disease. My mother is 75 years old. In January this year, she fell ill. After some examinations, we were told that she had a tumor in her brain. My mother lived in Kyushu [the southern part of Japan], but she had to move to Kanagawa Prefecture since the hospitals in Kyushu were not capable for treatment. Just the other day, she completed her treatment and we are very thankful that we were able to come to Master's lecture today.

My mother got married to the eldest son of a farm family when she was in her 20's and gave birth to three children. In her early 30's, she had problems in her ovaries and had to have them removed. Then, when she was 37, she had a surgery for breast cancer.

Since then she has been well and worked diligently as a farmer's wife, but in her later years she has been afflicted with this disease again.

My mother suffered twice from a serious illness in her 30s, during the most active period in child rearing and in supporting the family. Now, in her later years, she is afflicted with a brain disorder.

Could you please teach us why my mother had to get these diseases and the meaning of this for both my mother and the family in support of her?

There was something that did not match
The beautiful and feminine way of life

OKAWA:

Is your mother in this lecture hall right now?

[*The questioner's mother sitting at the rear makes a bow.*] Oh, hello. Some may refer to private matters, so this is difficult to ask, but we will not type this out. Could you tell me your name?

MOTHER OF Q3:

My name is xxx.

OKAWA:

And you are 75 years old. May I examine you? I do not know what is going to come out, so I will be careful with my words. You want to know why you are having these diseases.

[*He makes a fist with each hand and raises both as high as his shoulder. He starts a spiritual life reading of the mother from the podium. About 5 seconds of silence.*]

In regards to the diseases you had during the first half of your life, there seem to be some problems that your son [questioner] has not yet understood. Your son is not aware of it, but you have experienced a number of hardships. I believe there were conflicts. The two diseases, ovarian resection and breast cancer, are both actual conflicts and they are probably influenced by the farm work and your relationship with the family.

The fact that your diseases have deep connections to womanliness suggests that, during those times, you suffered the inability to lead the life you desired as a woman. This would sound rough, but I can hear your mind saying, "I was forced to work so hard like cattle as a wife." This feeling of being overworked like cattle does not accord to a woman's dignity or a beautiful way of living. This kind of thinking has caused the illness.

In order to go into further detail, I would have to point out specific relationship problems in your family. However, since everyone is going to hear it, I will refrain from it. I can see that some of your personal relationships did not work out so well. You are also unsatisfied that you were made to work like cattle. This is what there is in regards to the illnesses in your early days.

Diseases in the brain are caused by memories That we refuse to remember

[*To the questioner.*] Next, let us talk about your mother's illness in her later years. When she looks back on her life, it looks as though the length of time she has actually felt happy is very short. The more she looks back, the more she remembers memories of her being unhappy. In such cases, we try to erase those bad memories as a defense mechanism. This makes us prone to brain diseases such as dementia. In other words, she doesn't want to remember her past.

This thought of not wanting to remember the past creates a disease in the brain to make it forget many things. If the memories bring happiness, such disease will not be caused. However, if the memories she wants to forget outnumbers the ones she wants to remember, she will wish to forget her memories, making her prone to such illnesses.

I believe your mother experienced hardships for most of her life, with a very short time of being happy.

Present happiness can change
Past hardships into gold

As a method of treatment, the people around your mother must be more grateful for her. If the people around her are grateful for her and she is happy in her current situation, then all her hardships in the past will turn into happy memories.

I often say the following words—you cannot correct the past, but you can correct the future. You can change your future. As for the unchangeable past, if you learned your lesson through self-reflection, it is enough. So make efforts and sow good seeds to create a better future.

However, after reaching a certain age, some people may feel that they do not have much of a future left to change even if they plant seeds.

Well, for those people, I would like to tell them something that I have also mentioned in my book, *Healing Yourself* (Tokyo: Happy Science, 2008): "If you are happy right here and now, the adversities you experienced in the past will change to a golden hue." If you are happy now, it can be said that the adversities that you experienced were good whetstones for you to create the happiness that you have today.

Now, it is here that I think the people around the person should make efforts to help him or her feel happy in the current situation. Your mother's illness is most likely caused by a self-defense instinct because she doesn't want to remember her unhappy memories. What the people around her can do is to be kind to her and be grateful for her. Even if it is difficult to put into words, it is important that your family fills their heart with words of gratitude such as, "thank you mother" or "thank you grandmother" and wish for her to feel happiness at this current moment.

Her disease will reverse
When other people become grateful and kind

There is even a politician who suddenly gets "amnesia" when he is asked inconvenient questions [*audience laughs*]. Likewise, in most cases, those who get amnesia know something that will cause trouble to them if they remember it, making them prone to getting these types of illnesses. Having many bad memories would, of course, make us want to forget.

We, humans, have so-called "selective memory" which allows people to remember things that are convenient for them, but will try not to remember the things that puts them in an inconvenient situation. When this ability gets out of control, we start remembering a number of the bad memories.

However, if the brain functions in themselves start to malfunction, the brain will forget all the bad memories. In short, by damaging the functions of the brain, people become unable to understand anything. Just like morphinizing, it brings forth the effect of relieving pain.

In your mother's case, she has a sense of grudge toward her earlier life, since she feels that she was made to work like cattle. Additionally, she must have experienced some counter reaction toward this grudge as well. However, because there are parts of your mother's sufferings that you have not yet comprehended, you must understand that there are some things you cannot understand in regards to what your mother has gone through.

The underlying factor of your mother's current illness is the strong urge to suppress her unpleasant memories of the past. Therefore, please try to be grateful and kind and praise your mother as much as you can. This is what is important. By doing so, I believe your mother will gradually get better.

Additionally, as your mother becomes happy, the people around her must also become happy at the same time. The people around her must be happy, too; it is difficult to bring happiness to your mother alone. Hence, while having gratitude toward your mother, please make sure that you become happy yourself. If you have worries or problems and feel that you are unhappy, you must work to solve those problems. I have intentionally omitted a lot of details, but I hope you were able to understand what I have preached.

4

The Difference between People Who Are Cured Miraculously And the People Who Are Not

QUESTIONER 4:

Recently, my Dharma friend whom I conveyed the Truth to and became a member of Happy Science passed away from breast cancer. Although I participated in a ritual prayer, "Prayer for Recovery from Illness" on her behalf, she passed away. I am now reflecting on whether she passed away because I did not direct my heart toward her enough.

Among the members of Happy Science, there are those who are currently up and running after undergoing surgeries for breast cancer. Could you teach us why there are those who are miraculously cured from cancer while there are people who are not, as well as the difference between them?

People who experience the miracles Have some roles to fulfill

OKAWA:

I am very afraid that there aren't any determined set of rules around that. In this world, sometimes good people happen to die early, and though this may sound impolite, people who have poor reputation sometimes happen to live a long, healthy life. Like we all know, a lot of things in life do not go as we want them to.

There are times we are unable to solve the problem as to why a certain person gets a disease and dies in such a way by only focusing on this lifetime alone. If we focus on only this lifetime, we often tend to think, "This cannot be so." However, we can often find out the reason through conducting a past-life reading.

We must know that our life is not confined to this lifetime alone. If we go back in time and examine how people lived a couple of lifetimes back, we will find incidents that will make sense to us to what influenced the way the person died in this lifetime.

Usually, people who live in this world are unaware of this; therefore, they may become unsatisfied and have a sense of grudge toward heaven. However, every person is born into this world with their own challenge in life. If you focus on this life alone, you will not be able to fully understand why you were given this challenge. However, since everything is under the law of causality, there is nothing wrong in believing that there is some kind of meaning behind what we experience in this lifetime.

Therefore, as for people who experience miracles like recovering from cancer, we should understand that they are given an opportunity to accumulate virtues through the experience. Such people may contribute to increasing the number of people awakening to faith by bringing about their miraculous recovery from their diseases or their experience may become a driving power to carry out their missionary work successfully. They are given their roles and this kind of miracle sometimes occurs.

Some people get illnesses to redeem their karma

There are cases in which people, who were thought to be nice, pass away due to cancer. However, the reason becomes clear by reading their past lives. What I am about to speak of now has nothing to do with your friend, so please listen to it as a kind of fictional story.

For instance, even if a person made a good and righteous living in this life time, if we conduct a spiritual reading of the person's latest past life, he may have lived a selfish life by not taking enough care of the sick person in the family. So in order to redeem his karma, he becomes sick himself and die in an unfortunate way.

Also, there are people who undergo a countless number of surgical operations. In some of these cases, those people attacked and cut many people in their past life. This, in a larger ultimate sense, can also be a settlement of karma.

If people were born in the era of warriors and were involved in war, they may need to kill people and it may have been the right thing to do. There are times when these actions are for a good cause to protect the country or their family. However, there are times these matters remain as karma.

In such cases, people may experience various physical pains and suffer through illnesses in this lifetime. By experiencing these things in this lifetime, it offers us an opportunity to erase the feelings of regret toward hurting others in the past lives. After graduating this lifetime, what people did in their past lives will be erased and their karma will disappear because they have made up for it. Under such reasons, some people suffer through numerous surgeries.

Even if we cannot see the reasons in this life time, it would all make sense if we conduct a past-life reading. In this manner, the reason for your illnesses in this life time may be found in your past life. However, there will definitely be a next lifetime, so make sure you do not sow new seeds of negative karma which will manifest in a bad way in your future reincarnations.

No matter what kind situation or environment we are placed in, we must endeavor to live a great life. It is important to remember that we are leading a life that runs through the past, present and the future.

Hidden virtue is needed for miracles to happen

When miracles happen, there is an order of priority. High spirits wish to create miracles that are effective, as much as possible. The person must also have some sort of virtue. In most cases, people who experienced extraordinary miracles in this world have hidden virtues.

There are many things in life that do not go as we wish, but in the end we must remember that there is another world besides this one and that we cannot control everything.

However, the rules of cause and effect will never be inconsistent. If a person lives a righteous life, then they will be rewarded for sure. Not all Angels of Light succeeded in this world nor lived a healthy life without becoming ill. There are many who became heavily ill, who were assassinated or who went bankrupt, but they all returned to Heaven as Angels of Light.

Your life is not confined to this life time alone, so live righteously for the people and the society, with the perspective of happiness that carries from this world to the other.

Afterword

There are many people who deny the truth that they are the children of God and the children of Buddha, live with a materialistic perspective of life, and suffer from various illnesses. In a sense, it can be said that the sin of atheism or sin of unbelief is causing a reaction: countless amount of illnesses are being created.

Recently, a program aired on public broadcast about United States Armed Forces soldiers who lost their finger or their leg. In the program, when they rubbed a white powder which was made out of a pig's bladder, their finger or leg started to regenerate. It was aired as the "miracle powder" or "miracle method of regeneration."

However, I shall tell you. If the powder made from a pig's bladder can bring about such miracles, think about the miracles that will occur upon the words of El Cantare. Bring back the power to believe. Believe that you can regenerate your own body. Faith is stronger than illness.

Ryuho Okawa
Founder and CEO of the Happy Science Group
December 28, 2010

ABOUT THE AUTHOR

Founder and CEO of Happy Science Group.

Ryuho Okawa was born on July 7th 1956, in Tokushima, Japan. After graduating from the University of Tokyo with a law degree, he joined a Tokyo-based trading house. While working at its New York headquarters, he studied international finance at the Graduate Center of the City University of New York. In 1981, he attained Great Enlightenment and became aware that he is El Cantare with a mission to bring salvation to all humankind.

In 1986, he established Happy Science. It now has members in over 165 countries across the world, with more than 700 branches and temples as well as 10,000 missionary houses around the world.

He has given over 3,450 lectures (of which more than 150 are in English) and published over 3,000 books (of which more than 600 are Spiritual Interview Series), and many are translated into 40 languages. Along with *The Laws of the Sun* and *The Laws Of Messiah*, many of the books have become best sellers or million sellers. To date, Happy Science has produced 25 movies. The original story and original concept were given by the Executive Producer Ryuho Okawa. He has also composed music and written lyrics of over 450 pieces.

Moreover, he is the Founder of Happy Science University and Happy Science Academy (Junior and Senior High School), Founder and President of the Happiness Realization Party, Founder and Honorary Headmaster of Happy Science Institute of Government and Management, Founder of IRH Press Co., Ltd., and the Chairperson of NEW STAR PRODUCTION Co., Ltd. and ARI Production Co., Ltd.

WHAT IS EL CANTARE?

El Cantare means "the Light of the Earth," and is the Supreme God of the Earth who has been guiding humankind since the beginning of Genesis. He is whom Jesus called Father and Muhammad called Allah, and is *Ame-no-Mioya-Gami*, Japanese Father God. Different parts of El Cantare's core consciousness have descended to Earth in the past, once as Alpha and another as Elohim. His branch spirits, such as Shakyamuni Buddha and Hermes, have descended to Earth many times and helped to flourish many civilizations. To unite various religions and to integrate various fields of study in order to build a new civilization on Earth, a part of the core consciousness has descended to Earth as Master Ryuho Okawa.

Alpha is a part of the core consciousness of El Cantare who descended to Earth around 330 million years ago. Alpha preached Earth's Truths to harmonize and unify Earth-born humans and space people who came from other planets.

Elohim is a part of El Cantare's core consciousness who descended to Earth around 150 million years ago. He gave wisdom, mainly on the differences of light and darkness, good and evil.

Ame-no-Mioya-Gami (Japanese Father God) is the Creator God and the Father God who appears in the ancient literature, *Hotsuma Tsutae*. It is believed that He descended on the foothills of Mt. Fuji about 30,000 years ago and built the Fuji dynasty, which is the root of the Japanese civilization. With justice as the central pillar, Ame-no-Mioya-Gami's teachings spread to ancient civilizations of other countries in the world.

Shakyamuni Buddha was born as a prince into the Shakya Clan in India around 2,600 years ago. When he was 29 years old, he renounced the world and sought enlightenment. He later attained Great Enlightenment and founded Buddhism.

Hermes is one of the 12 Olympian gods in Greek mythology, but the spiritual Truth is that he taught the teachings of love and progress around 4,300 years ago that became the origin of the current Western civilization. He is a hero that truly existed.

Ophealis was born in Greece around 6,500 years ago and was the leader who took an expedition to as far as Egypt. He is the God of miracles, prosperity, and arts, and is known as Osiris in the Egyptian mythology.

Rient Arl Croud was born as a king of the ancient Incan Empire around 7,000 years ago and taught about the mysteries of the mind. In the heavenly world, he is responsible for the interactions that take place between various planets.

Thoth was an almighty leader who built the golden age of the Atlantic civilization around 12,000 years ago. In the Egyptian mythology, he is known as god Thoth.

Ra Mu was a leader who built the golden age of the civilization of Mu around 17,000 years ago. As a religious leader and a politician, he ruled by uniting religion and politics.

ABOUT HAPPY SCIENCE

Happy Science is a global movement that empowers individuals to find purpose and spiritual happiness and to share that happiness with their families, societies, and the world. With more than 12 million members around the world, Happy Science aims to increase awareness of spiritual truths and expand our capacity for love, compassion, and joy so that together we can create the kind of world we all wish to live in.

Activities at Happy Science are based on the Principle of Happiness (Love, Wisdom, Self-Reflection, and Progress). This principle embraces worldwide philosophies and beliefs, transcending boundaries of culture and religions.

Love teaches us to give ourselves freely without expecting anything in return; it encompasses giving, nurturing, and forgiving.

Wisdom leads us to the insights of spiritual truths, and opens us to the true meaning of life and the will of God (the universe, the highest power, Buddha).

Self-Reflection brings a mindful, nonjudgmental lens to our thoughts and actions to help us find our truest selves—the essence of our souls—and deepen our connection to the highest power. It helps us attain a clean and peaceful mind and leads us to the right life path.

Progress emphasizes the positive, dynamic aspects of our spiritual growth—actions we can take to manifest and spread happiness around the world. It's a path that not only expands our soul growth, but also furthers the collective potential of the world we live in.

PROGRAMS AND EVENTS

The doors of Happy Science are open to all. We offer a variety of programs and events, including self-exploration and self-growth programs, spiritual seminars, meditation and contemplation sessions, study groups, and book events.

Our programs are designed to:
* Deepen your understanding of your purpose and meaning in life
* Improve your relationships and increase your capacity to love unconditionally
* Attain peace of mind, decrease anxiety and stress, and feel positive
* Gain deeper insights and a broader perspective on the world
* Learn how to overcome life's challenges
  ... and much more.

For more information, visit happy-science.org.

CONTACT INFORMATION

Happy Science is a worldwide organization with branches and temples around the globe. For a comprehensive list, visit the worldwide directory at *happy-science.org*. The following are some of the many Happy Science locations:

UNITED STATES AND CANADA

New York
79 Franklin St., New York, NY 10013, USA
Phone: 1-212-343-7972
Fax: 1-212-343-7973
Email: ny@happy-science.org
Website: happyscience-usa.org

New Jersey
66 Hudson St., #2R, Hoboken, NJ 07030, USA
Phone: 1-201-313-0127
Email: nj@happy-science.org
Website: happyscience-usa.org

Chicago
2300 Barrington Rd., Suite #400,
Hoffman Estates, IL 60169, USA
Phone: 1-630-937-3077
Email: chicago@happy-science.org
Website: happyscience-usa.org

Florida
5208 8th St., Zephyrhills, FL 33542, USA
Phone: 1-813-715-0000
Fax: 1-813-715-0010
Email: florida@happy-science.org
Website: happyscience-usa.org

Atlanta
1874 Piedmont Ave., NE Suite 360-C
Atlanta, GA 30324, USA
Phone: 1-404-892-7770
Email: atlanta@happy-science.org
Website: happyscience-usa.org

San Francisco
525 Clinton St.
Redwood City, CA 94062, USA
Phone & Fax: 1-650-363-2777
Email: sf@happy-science.org
Website: happyscience-usa.org

Los Angeles
1590 E. Del Mar Blvd., Pasadena, CA
91106, USA
Phone: 1-626-395-7775
Fax: 1-626-395-7776
Email: la@happy-science.org
Website: happyscience-usa.org

Orange County
16541 Gothard St. Suite 104
Huntington Beach, CA 92647
Phone: 1-714-659-1501
Email: oc@happy-science.org
Website: happyscience-usa.org

San Diego
7841 Balboa Ave. Suite #202
San Diego, CA 92111, USA
Phone: 1-626-395-7775
Fax: 1-626-395-7776
E-mail: sandiego@happy-science.org
Website: happyscience-usa.org

Hawaii
Phone: 1-808-591-9772
Fax: 1-808-591-9776
Email: hi@happy-science.org
Website: happyscience-usa.org

Kauai
3343 Kanakolu Street, Suite 5
Lihue, HI 96766, USA
Phone: 1-808-822-7007
Fax: 1-808-822-6007
Email: kauai-hi@happy-science.org
Website: happyscience-usa.org

Toronto

845 The Queensway
Etobicoke, ON M8Z 1N6, Canada
Phone: 1-416-901-3747
Email: toronto@happy-science.org
Website: happy-science.ca

Vancouver

#201-2607 East 49th Avenue,
Vancouver, BC, V5S 1J9, Canada
Phone: 1-604-437-7735
Fax: 1-604-437-7764
Email: vancouver@happy-science.org
Website: happy-science.ca

INTERNATIONAL

Tokyo

1-6-7 Togoshi, Shinagawa,
Tokyo, 142-0041, Japan
Phone: 81-3-6384-5770
Fax: 81-3-6384-5776
Email: tokyo@happy-science.org
Website: happy-science.org

Seoul

74, Sadang-ro 27-gil,
Dongjak-gu, Seoul, Korea
Phone: 82-2-3478-8777
Fax: 82-2-3478-9777
Email: korea@happy-science.org
Website: happyscience-korea.org

London

3 Margaret St.
London, W1W 8RE United Kingdom
Phone: 44-20-7323-9255
Fax: 44-20-7323-9344
Email: eu@happy-science.org
Website: www.happyscience-uk.org

Taipei

No. 89, Lane 155, Dunhua N. Road,
Songshan District, Taipei City 105, Taiwan
Phone: 886-2-2719-9377
Fax: 886-2-2719-5570
Email: taiwan@happy-science.org
Website: happyscience-tw.org

Sydney

516 Pacific Highway, Lane Cove North,
2066 NSW, Australia
Phone: 61-2-9411-2877
Fax: 61-2-9411-2822
Email: sydney@happy-science.org

Kuala Lumpur

No 22A, Block 2, Jalil Link Jalan Jalil
Jaya 2, Bukit Jalil 57000,
Kuala Lumpur, Malaysia
Phone: 60-3-8998-7877
Fax: 60-3-8998-7977
Email: malaysia@happy-science.org
Website: happyscience.org.my

Sao Paulo

Rua. Domingos de Morais 1154,
Vila Mariana, Sao Paulo SP
CEP 04010-100, Brazil
Phone: 55-11-5088-3800
Email: sp@happy-science.org
Website: happyscience.com.br

Kathmandu

Kathmandu Metropolitan City,
Ward No. 15, Ring Road, Kimdol,
Sitapaila Kathmandu, Nepal
Phone: 977-1-427-2931
Email: nepal@happy-science.org

Jundiai

Rua Congo, 447, Jd. Bonfiglioli
Jundiai-CEP, 13207-340, Brazil
Phone: 55-11-4587-5952
Email: jundiai@happy-science.org

Kampala

Plot 877 Rubaga Road, Kampala
P.O. Box 34130 Kampala, UGANDA
Phone: 256-79-4682-121
Email: uganda@happy-science.org

ABOUT HS PRESS

HS Press is an imprint of IRH Press Co., Ltd. IRH Press Co., Ltd., based in Tokyo, was founded in 1987 as a publishing division of Happy Science. IRH Press publishes religious and spiritual books, journals, magazines and also operates broadcast and film production enterprises. For more information, visit *okawabooks.com*.

Follow us on:

f Facebook: Okawa Books   **Instagram: OkawaBooks

▶ Youtube: Okawa Books   Twitter: Okawa Books

P Pinterest: Okawa Books   **g** Goodreads: Ryuho Okawa

——— **NEWSLETTER** ———

To receive book related news, promotions and events, please subscribe to our newsletter below.

∂ eepurl.com/bsMeJj

——— **AUDIO / VISUAL MEDIA** ———

YOUTUBE

PODCAST

Introduction of Ryuho Okawa's titles; topics ranging from self-help, current affairs, spirituality, religion, and the universe.

BOOKS BY RYUHO OKAWA

THE LAWS OF WISDOM
SHINE YOUR DIAMOND WITHIN

This book guides you along the path on how to acquire wisdom, so that you can break through any wall you are or will confront in your life or in your business. By reading this book, you will be able to avoid getting lost in the flood of information and, going beyond the level of just amassing knowledge, be able to come up with many great ideas, make effective planning and strategy and develop your leadership while receiving good inspiration.

THE LAWS OF PERSEVERANCE
REVERSING YOUR COMMON SENSE

"No matter how much you suffer, the Truth will gradually shine forth as you continue to endure hardships. Therefore, simply strengthen your mind and keep making constant efforts in times of endurance, however ordinary they may be. "
-From Postscript

THE LAWS OF GREAT ENLIGHTENMENT
ALWAYS WALK WITH BUDDHA

In this modern society, we often find ourselves unable to forgive someone and maintain a peaceful mind. However, there are ways to lead a stress-free life and enjoy happiness from within. This book offers the practical approaches to achieve it. By understanding the Buddhist concept "enlightenment," you will gain the power to forgive sins and get to know how to be the master of your own mind.

For a complete list of books, visit okawabooks.com

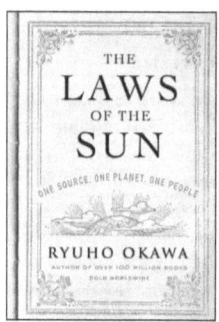

THE LAWS OF THE SUN
ONE SOURCE, ONE PLANET, ONE PEOPLE

IMAGINE IF YOU COULD ASK GOD why He created this world and what spiritual laws He used to shape us—and everything around us. If we could understand His designs and intentions, we could discover what our goals in life should be and whether our actions move us closer to those goals or farther away.

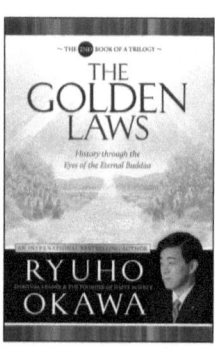

THE GOLDEN LAWS
HISTORY THROUGH THE EYES OF THE ETERNAL BUDDHA

The Golden Laws reveals how Buddha's Plan has been unfolding on earth, and outlines five thousand years of the secret history of humankind. Once we understand the true course of history, we cannot help but become aware of the significance of our spiritual mission in the present age.

THE NINE DIMENSIONS
UNVEILING THE LAWS OF ETERNITY

This book is a window into the mind of our loving God, who encourages us to grow into greater angels. It reveals His deepest intentions, answering the timely question of why He conceived such a colorful medley of religions, philosophies, sciences, arts, and other forms of expression.

For a complete list of books, visit okawabooks.com

SPIRITUAL WORLD 101

A GUIDE TO A SPIRITUALLY HAPPY LIFE

This book is a spiritual guidebook that will answer all your questions about the spiritual world, with illustrations and diagrams explaining about your guardian spirit and the secrets of God and Buddha. By reading this book, you will be able to understand the true meaning of life and find happiness in everyday life.

BASICS OF EXORCISM

HOW TO PROTECT YOU AND YOUR FAMILY FROM EVIL SPIRITS

No matter how much time progresses, demons are real. Spiritual screen against curses - the truth of exorcism as told by the author who possesses the six great supernatural powers - The essence of exorcism as a result of more than 5000 rounds of exorcist experience!

HEALING FROM WITHIN

LIFE-CHANGING KEYS TO CALM, SPIRITUAL, AND HEALTHY LIVING

The true causes and remedies for various illnesses that modern medicine doesn't know how to cure are revealed in this book. By following the steps that are suggested here, you will gain new perspective on the relationship between mind and body.

For a complete list of books, visit okawabooks.com

IN LOVE WITH THE SUN

SPIRITUAL MESSAGES FROM GODDESS GAIA

After 600 million years, people shall know the true genesis. The true story when the earth was born, the guiding concept of the earth, the mechanism of creating life on Earth. And the future that human beings has to seek, these secrets are now revealed by the spiritual message from Goddess Gaia, who supported the creation of Earth civilization by Alpha, the God of origin.

THE ART OF BUSINESS REVITALIZATION

MANAGEMENT WISDOM FROM JACK WELCH, CARLOS GHOSN, AND BILL GATES

What management philosophies or secret to creating products that become global standards or human resources management and education philosophies have they drawn upon to keep their companies at the top? This book reveals the secrets to their achievements.

MOTHER TERESA'S CURRENT CALLING IN HEAVEN

THE SAINT OF THE GUTTERS DELIVERS HER EXPERIENCES OF GOD, HEAVEN, AND OUR MISSION

In this spiritual interview, Mother Teresa's spirit talks about her astonishing discoveries about God, Heaven, and the mission that people on earth should aim to fulfill through life. She reveals that the other world is a vast place with many levels of angels, that Heaven and Hell exist, and that the reality of the human being is the soul.

For a complete list of books in the Spiritual Interview Series, visit spiritualinterview.com